A Guidebook for Teaching ENGLISH AS A SECOND LANGUAGE

BEVERLY S. WATTENMAKER

VIRGINIA WILSON

Allyn and Bacon, Inc. Boston • London • Sydney • Toronto

_195846_

This book is part of A GUIDEBOOK FOR TEACHING Series

Portions of this book also appear in _A Guidebook for Teaching Foreign Language: Spanish, French, and German_ by Beverly S. Wattenmaker and Virginia Wilson, Copyright © 1980 by Allyn and Bacon, Inc.

The Reproduction Pages contained within may be reproduced for use with this text, provided such reproductions bear copyright notice, but may not be reproduced in any form for any other purpose without permission from the copyright owner.

We are grateful to the following for permission to reproduce copyright material: "Ken Wilson and Longman Group Ltd. for 'Present Continuous Baby' from _Mister Monday and Other Songs for the Teaching of English_ and 'I'm Looking Forward to the Day' from _Goodbye Rainbow_ by Ken Wilson, reprinted by permission of the author and Longman Group Ltd."

Library of Congress Cataloging in Publication Data

Wattenmaker, Beverly S
  A guidebook for teaching English as a second language.

  (A Guidebook for teaching series)
  Bibliography: p.
  Includes index.
  1. English language—Study and teaching—Foreign students. I. Wilson, Virginia, joint author. II. Title. III. Series: Guidebook for teaching series.
PE1128.A2W27   420ˑ.7   79–28729
ISBN 0–205–06976–2

Managing Editor: Robert Roen
Series Editor: David Pallai
Production Editor: Sandy Stanewick
Preparation Buyer: Sharlene Queenan

Printed in the United States of America

About the authors

Beverly S. Wattenmaker received her M.A. in Spanish from Case Western Reserve. She has been Foreign Language Coordinator of the Kenston Public Schools and has taught Spanish on both the middle and high school levels. She has been a member of the Values Clarification Network of leaders in humanistic education, has taught workshops on foreign language in the United States, Canada, and Mexico, and has co-authored several books in the field.

Virginia Wilson received her M.A. in Cross-Cultural Education and Language Education at the University of Alaska, where she has taught. She has been a member of the Values Clarification Network of leaders in humanistic education, has co-authored several books in the field, and has taught foreign language workshops in the United States, Canada, and Mexico.

Gene Stanford, Consulting Editor for the Guidebook for Teaching Series, received his Ph.D. and his M.A. from the University of Colorado. Dr. Stanford has served as Associate Professor of Education and Director of Teacher Education Programs at Utica College of Syracuse University and is a member of the National Council of Teachers of English and the International Council on Education for Teaching. Dr. Stanford is the author and co-author of several books, among them, *A Guidebook for Teaching Composition, A Guidebook for Teaching Creative Writing, A Guidebook for Teaching about the English Language,* and *Human Interaction in Education,* all published by Allyn and Bacon, Inc.

Contents

Preface

Before you read beyond this sentence, think for a moment about why you are reading this book and what your real concerns are for your language classes.

Perhaps we can share some of our concerns, and help bring into focus what we hope to accomplish.

1. How can we help our students become more involved in learning a new language?
2. How can we create a feeling of relevance and excitement about grammar?
3. How can we put a little more fun and a little less drudgery into teaching a new language?
4. How can we relate more effectively to our students and their needs?
5. How can we build interest in learning a new language?
6. How can we help our students to appreciate and accept each other—an important goal itself and the necessary first step toward appreciating other people and other cultures?

In the past few years, we have come up with some answers to these questions that have made our lives more fun, have gotten our students more involved, and have made language teaching a center of attention in our school. We have slowly earned the respect of our administration, of other teachers, and of the student body for the relevance and excitement of our program.

We hope to help you fill the gap between the textbook and the creative use of language in real communication. You will find some of the answers in this book, but we don't wish to overpromise—you won't find all the answers. Your own hard work, involvement, and probably courage may be more important than what we offer you. We are, however, excited about sharing with you some of the activities and, more importantly, the processes that we have found effective. We think you will find them interesting and productive in making language learning a meaningful and worthwhile experience for your students and for yourself. We hope that you will find them a guide and also a stimulus to do more than you may have thought possible.

We began teaching foreign language at a small high school on the outskirts of Cleveland, Ohio. The Kenston School District is a conglomerate of suburban/rural/poverty areas with a diverse student body, including many vocational students who are not college bound. We learned the hard way that for most students the academic experience of learning a foreign language is not motivation enough. We discovered, however, that students *are motivated to learn about themselves,* and that we can effectively combine learning a language with learning about ourselves. We have worked out ways to coordinate human development experiences with grammar teaching activities, to get out of the textbook and into personal communication in an environment where people feel accepted and secure. Now we find students using their new language as a tool for meaningful communication. They are responding to us and to each other with sympathetic interest and concern. We have shared these ideas with teachers in workshops across the United States, in Canada, and in Mexico; and we have discovered that they, like us, find more success and joy in teaching and learning in this way.

We are happy to be able to share these ideas with you.

This is a guidebook for teaching communication in any language. The ideas and techniques for teaching communication are demonstrated in actual lesson models in the two guidebooks in this series. *A Guidebook for Teaching Foreign Language* has detailed sections for teaching Spanish, French, and German. *A Guidebook for Teaching English as a Second Language* has a detailed section for teaching English. Restricted by the size of the books to giving detailed plans in only these four languages, we must ask teachers of other languages to translate the activities and adapt them to their own objectives. You may want to acquaint yourself with the activities in all the language sections. Although there are similar activities in the various language sections, there are different ones as well. Teachers of one language can find new ideas by reading the other language chapters or by discussing the suggested activities with teachers of those languages.

Each language-teaching chapter includes:

1. A sequence of behavior objectives and corresponding grammar objectives,
2. Teaching and communication exercises directed toward the achievement of each objective,
3. Suggestions for evaluation,
4. Annotated lists of resources.

Appendix A lists the names and addresses of the publishers of the selected resources. Appendix B contains the Reproduction Pages, which you can copy for worksheets and learning activities for your students. You can photocopy them or make masters for duplication; or you can make transparencies for use with the overhead projector (saving hours of preparation time). Appendix C provides a feedback form, because we want to know what has been helpful and what has worked for you.

Some of the exercises can be used in a tightly structured teaching situation in which correction has an important place in helping to define grammar concepts. The exercises are most effective, however, in promoting and maintaining a real-life, nonjudgmental environment. In this way, the target language becomes a relevant tool for meaningful and important communication, rather than merely a learning objective.

A little classroom experience with this method quickly proves how much more we "get out" of students by talking with them about who they and we are and what all of us are going to be doing. This is *real communication* and creates far more involvement and learning than talking about the pen on the table or the street cleaner in Paris or the soldier in Spain. Our emphasis is on interaction and working together—students and teacher working as a group, learning and sharing.

We thank Dr. Michael Krauss, of the University of Alaska, who provided advice on the linguistic analysis underlying the presentation of the sound and writing systems, and also our English language students at the University of Alaska in Fairbanks and at the English Language Services Language Center in Cleveland, Ohio, for all that they have taught us. Jim Wattenmaker gave his time, expertise, and energy in clarifying, advising, and editing. Stacey Wilson gave confident support.

Welcome! Please share your own experience with us. We would like to hear from you—your concerns and your successes.

Grammar Guide

Introduction

We find that students learn better and faster when involved in real communication. Classes are more fun, more interesting, more productive. As teachers, we feel more successful when we involve our students in the natural use of the language instead of directing a dialog or asking them the personal questions at the end of the unit. Some structured classroom activities, however, are needed *to teach grammar* in an ordered sequence of basic functions of the language from personal pronouns to all tenses and moods of verbs; and *to free people to talk and interact* in a group dynamics situation, which develops a sense of mutual trust and feelings of confidence in oneself and in others.

Activities to teach grammar and provide for friendly interaction are the focus of this book. Students become excited when they are involved in meaningful language use in class rather than in working from the textbook or doing worksheets. They quickly learn to think in the language and to generate new phrases and sentences rather than just repeating the ones they have heard.

We use textbooks and prepared audiovisual materials as resources to extend the students' understanding beyond the classroom and their own experiences. When we plan a lesson, we choose a few communication and teaching activities to complement whatever textbook and audiovisual materials we decide to use. You can do the same by coordinating the language teaching activities that follow with your own course objectives and textbook.

1. Determine the objective of a given lesson.
2. Find a similar objective in the list at the beginning of the language chapter or in the grammar index.
3. Look in the language chapter for the grammar topic with the same number as the objective.
4. Choose activities from those described under that topic.

We find that using the communication activities as the primary teaching tool and the textbook as backup works best for us. There is no right way, however, and we encourage you to experiment and work out what feels most comfortable for you and your class. You may change the emphasis as you gain confidence in these activities or as your objectives vary.

We use several textbooks, and refer even beginning students to other resources: dictionaries, reference grammars, graded readers. Students like the textbook as a handy reference for answers to questions like these:

- How do you say . .?
- Why do you say it that way?
- How do you conjugate . . .?

They can also use the textbook for dialog and paragraph models, for reading, and for practicing exercises with each other when they are provided with an answer key. How to use the textbook by themselves becomes more important when teachers stop being audioversions of the book. Students discover that books are sources to learn from by studying, while teachers and other students are sources to learn from by listening and talking.

Real communication in the language classroom is more fun for students and teachers. There may be more work involved in planning lessons, but it pays off in increased student interest and learning.

1

Techniques for Teaching Communication

Human beings are by nature social. We must communicate in order to live, not only on the practical level of satisfying physical needs but also on the more abstract level of satisfying psychological needs. Fortunately for us as language teachers, language is the most essential tool for meeting those needs.

We can concentrate on freeing our students and ourselves from limitations on our ability to communicate and on creating an environment that invites real communication. We are teaching skills that students *want* to learn, and so they provide their own motivation. They will communicate in order to satisfy their needs for security, identification with a group, recognition, and personal satisfaction, not just to get a credit.

In this way, the student's motivation involves the total person. The activities that we suggest should also involve the total person—physically, intellectually, emotionally, and socially. Communication in the classroom thus becomes *R*elevant, *E*njoyable, *A*nd *L*ive—that is, *REAL*.

People learning a new language are easily frustrated by how long they think it will take to learn enough to communicate freely. *It is important, therefore, to structure the learning in such a way that successful, and in some way satisfying, communication takes place at every step of the learning process.* We need to begin with simple language that we can immediately use and build on. This is why with this method we begin by teaching in any language the equivalent of:

I'm Beverly Wattenmaker. Who are you?
I'm a woman. I'm a teacher. I'm a mother. Who are you?

We used to begin with **"My name is. . . ."** But then we were stuck. We had nowhere to go except to start all over again with something new.

In each of the following language chapters, we suggest a sequence of basic grammar concepts and describe specific activities for teaching the concepts and using them in real communication.

In this chapter we describe methods and techniques for putting the activities into operation:

- Direct method
- Audiovisual method

- Communication strategies
- Forming small groups
- Reflective listening
- Real-life experiences
- Writing
- Reading
- Evaluation

Examples of foreign or second language activities that can be translated for teaching other languages are printed with the same boldface type that distinguishes student activities in the language chapters. There is nothing exclusive about the different techniques; they can be combined in a single class period or at any time during the course of study. Each has its place. The direct method is excellent for teaching grammar. We like the audiovisual method for teaching the understanding of words and their function and extended vocabulary. Real communication helps people say what they want.

Because so much of this book is devoted to the description of processes and activities, we are concerned that you may lose sight of our focus on attitudes. What we do in the classroom is not really as important as how we feel. When both the teacher's and the students' attitudes are open, trusting, and nonjudgmental, almost any activity provides a solid learning experience. The most valuable activities are those that nurture accepting attitudes.

DIRECT METHOD

The essential element of the direct method is the learning of grammar and vocabulary through meaningful use so that understanding is quickly internalized by means of personal experience. Students understand first through demonstration in the classroom and later through illustrations and context in books.

We design lesson plans that make transpositions from basic, simple declarative sentences, to questions, imperatives, and negative statements involving the first, second, and third persons. You may include plural forms, although it is better to postpone their use until the students have assimilated the singular forms.

Example of Oral Grammar Manipulation

Objective: To use the verb **see.**

Sit with the students in a circle.

Teacher:	Student:
I see the map. Mike, do you see it?	**Yes, I see it.**
Ask Judy if she sees it.	**Judy, do you see it?**
	Yes, I see it.
Does Judy see the map?	**Yes, she sees it.**
Susan, what do you see?	**I see ⎯⎯⎯⎯⎯.**

We can rely on students' natural ability to make transformations from first to second person, question to answer. The teacher is the resource person, supplying new words and giving feedback on correct usage.

Caleb Gattegno (see resources at the end of this chapter) has developed a highly stylized direct method, which he calls "The Silent Way." He uses Cuisenaire rods (1 cm square rods in lengths of 1 to 10 cm, each a different color) to create linguistic situations. He presents only a few words as models and lets students do the talking.

Example of "The Silent Way"

Objective: To use adjectives describing color.

1. Pick up the rods one by one, saying each time, **"A rod."** Then indicate that students are to do the same.
2. Pick up a red rod and put it down, saying, **"A red rod."** Pick up a black rod, saying, **"A black rod."** Signal a student to touch and identify the first one and then the second. Have all students do the same. Continue with more colors.
3. Say, **"Pick up a red rod."** Place a student's hand on the rod, closing his or her fingers over it and lifting the rod with the student's hand to show the meaning. Say, **"Pick up a blue one."** Signal students to give each other similar commands.

Learning with rods is by no means limited to size, number, and color. Using rods imaginatively, students and teachers can set up graphic representations of situations they want to talk about. Look at these examples:

- Standing three rods on the table, I point to each one saying:

  This is me. This is my brother. He is older than I am. This is my sister. She is younger than I.

  Students reach eagerly for rods to describe their own families.
- Laying out rods like a floor plan, we describe our rooms:

  This is my bedroom. To the right of the door is the desk. My bed is next to the window. On each side there is a table.
- Students set up a village and describe the setting of a story:

  Here is the town. The big house is the military headquarters. On both sides of the muddy street are fences and small houses. At the end there is an old shack standing on the shore of the sea.

Gattegno is telling us:

- Be quiet and let students talk.
- Put manipulative materials in the students' hands for the total physical response of touching, feeling, thinking, and talking that assures learning and remembering.

- Let students use their natural powers for extracting words from a stream of sound, making transformations rather than repeating what they hear, and abstracting meaning from words.

The direct method is fast and efficient. Students can quickly learn grammar concepts that appear complicated on paper but are relatively simple in practice.

AUDIOVISUAL METHOD

Most of us would agree that the ideal way to learn a foreign language is to be immersed in the foreign culture, to hear native speakers use the language, to discover meaning from gestures and emotional clues, to analyze the way words express meaning, and then to use the language. We can approximate this in the classroom by using pictures of cultural situations, with native dialogs recorded on tape and a special question-answer technique for analyzing the structure of the dialog sentences.

The dialogs are not to be memorized. They are actually a data bank for functional vocabulary and meaningful grammar use. Students gain access to the data through the teacher's carefully planned questions, which help students discover the meaning and function of each word in the sentence.

Questions like these help to define the grammar of any language:

Who is this?

What is this?

What is ___she___ doing? What did ___she___ do?

What is ___she___ going to do?

Who is ___she___ doing it to?

How? When? Where? Why?

These questions can be used individually or in small groups when reading a well-illustrated book, or they can be used in large groups with projected pictures and a recorded dialog. Audiovisual materials consisting of dialog that gradually introduces the grammar concepts and the most basic vocabulary of a language, along with drawings to illustrate the mood, actions and thoughts of the speaker are available (see the resources at the end of this chapter). You can create dialog to go with slides or other filmstrips, or make a transparency with your own pictures and dialog.

Teachers like this method because we can use the target language almost exclusively. We can talk instead of drilling. We can use the pictures and affective reactions of the speakers to help students understand the culture. We appreciate the intellectual and social involvement of the students, and we delight in students' fluent and creative use of the language.

Students like being able to function quickly in the new language. Amazingly, they soon think in the language instead of translating. They discover that they learn from mistakes—their own and others.

Note that when students are actively involved in discovery and meaningful use of the language, this method is successful and exciting. For those students who never feel the joy of discovery, however, the questions may be frustrating. It is important to be sensitive to what students

Example of Question-Answer Technique with Audiovisual Materials

Objective: To understand sentence structure and meaning.

1. Play the entire recorded dialog while showing the pictures.
2. Go back to the first picture, play its audio, and ask the following questions that isolate each word in the sentence and help indicate its function.

Tape:

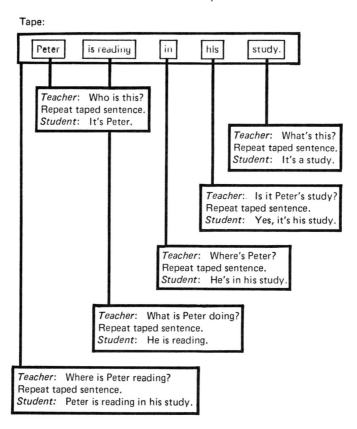

3. Students repeat the entire sentence only after they have talked about and understood its parts.

are learning and feeling and to make sure that all of them have opportunities to be successful—if not in one kind of activity, then in another.

Here are some suggestions for setting up the classroom and for using the audiovisual method:

1. Arrange the room with the screen and tape recorder on one side, the projector on the opposite side, and enough space for the teacher to move freely in between. Seat students in rows facing each other. Have a student operate the projector.

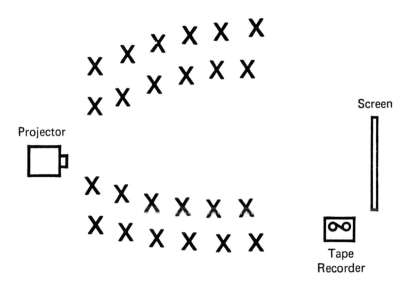

2. Use a tape player with quick replay and a pause control. Avoid players with noisy on-off switches. Or use a card player like Language Master or Voxcom.

3. Write out a detailed lesson plan, with questions and anticipated student responses for each sentence of the dialog. See the example below and models in the topic for giving directions in each language chapter.

4. Ask the questions quickly, repeating the same question to several students often enough to assure understanding.

5. When a student can't answer, ask another question that may help him or her think of an answer. If the student is still unable to answer, go on to another. Be sure to return, however, to give that first student the chance to answer.

6. Finally, apply the grammar and vocabulary learned to real-life situations.

Example of Explaining an Audiovisual Dialog

Objective: To learn to give directions for going someplace.

Make a transparency using Reproduction Page 1. Have native speakers or advanced students record the dialog.

1. *Tourist (a man):*   Excuse me, please. Where is the post office?
2. *Clerk (a woman):*   Go out that door and turn right.
3. *Clerk:*   Go straight ahead for two blocks.
4. *Clerk:*   Turn left at the traffic light.
5. *Clerk:*   When you get to the drugstore, cross the street.
6. *Clerk:*   The post office is across from the drugstore.
7. *Tourist:*   Thank you very much. Good-bye.

Lesson Plan for Line 1

Tape: **Excuse me, please. Where is the post office?**

Teacher:	Repeat Tape	Student:
What is this? (Point to post office.)	tape	**It's the post office.**
Does he (the tourist) know where the post office is?	tape	**No, he doesn't know where the post office is.**

Teacher:	Repeat Tape	Student:
Does she (the clerk) know where it is?	tape	**Yes, she knows where it is.**
___**Carlos**___ **, you are the tourist. Ask the clerk where the post office is.**	tape	**Excuse me, please. Where is the post office?**

Lesson Plan for Line 2

Tape: **Go out that door and turn right.**

Teacher:	Repeat Tape	Student:
What is this? (Point to door.)	tape	**It's a door.**
Is the man coming in or going out the door? (Point to drawing.)	tape	**He's going out the door.**
Is he going to turn right or left?	tape	**He's going to turn right.**
Tell him to turn right.	tape	**Turn right.**
___**Kasuko**___ **, you are the clerk. Tell him where to go.**	tape	**Go out that door and turn right.**

Lesson Plans for Lines 3 through 6

Continue with similar questions and answers.

COMMUNICATION STRATEGIES

To establish real communication it is important to help the class function in the target language so that, from the beginning, the new language is a valuable tool for the meaningful exchange of information, ideas, and feelings. Teachers are learning a great deal from psychologists and counselors about the powerful role of group dynamics in the function of our classes. Group interaction provides a stimulus for learning and working. Adapting simple communication strategies—such as interviews, conversation circles, and values clarification—to the specific vocabulary and grammar capabilities of students gives them the confidence and motivation to use the language in a meaningful way.

Specific grammar objectives are used here to illustrate each communication strategy. Many more objectives with activities are suggested in the language chapters that follow.

Conversation Circles

Psychologists Bessell and Palomares (see the resources at the end of the chapter) use a structured way for sharing experiences, thoughts, and feelings in order to help children develop good mental health through self-awareness, mastery, and social interaction.

A group of no more than sixteen people sit together in a circle. Circle seating can be difficult to arrange. It is important, however, because to share experiences, feelings, and ideas, students and teachers have to be able to see each other's faces. (When students are asked to respond to questions that involve a personal answer, and they are not sitting so that they can see as well as listen to each other, very little meaningful communication takes place. Instead it is just another teacher-student interchange; the rest of the group does not feel a sense of involvement.)

The leader starts by announcing a topic or question, and students take turns responding or passing if they choose. It is not a discussion, but simply sharing and listening. When all who want to respond have done so, the leader initiates a process of recalling the answers, addressing each participant personally by name. Other members of the group help and continue the recall until everyone is remembered. This makes people feel good, feel accepted. (And the language teacher can't help thinking, "What an exciting way to conjugate a verb!")

Example of a Conversation Circle

Objective: To use the verb **have** with personal meaning.

Leader starts:

—**¿Qué tienes que te hace sentir a gusto?** (*What do you have that makes you feel good?*)

—**Tengo una motocicleta.** (*I have a motorcycle.*)

—**Tengo mi perro. Me siento contenta.** (*I have my dog. I feel happy.*)

—**Tengo un perro también. Lisa y yo tenemos perros.** (*I have my dog too. Lisa and I have dogs.*)

When everyone who wants to has answered, the leader begins to recall:

—**Lisa, tienes tu perro. Te sientes contenta.** (*Lisa, you have your dog. You feel happy.*)

Students continue:

—**Bob, tienes tu motocicleta.** (*Bob, you have your motorcycle.*)

—**Maria y Lisa, ustedes tienen los perros.** (*Maria and Lisa, you have your dogs.*)

The topics for conversation circles are quite simple. They are little more than grammar questions with a touch of feeling. The answers are personal but, as you can see in the example above, quite ordinary, even superficial. There is no pressure to go any deeper. However, the structure of the conversation circle—each person sharing, no discussion, reflective listening—creates a warm climate that sometimes invites more meaningful involvement. In a racially integrated group, one day, a girl looked down at her hand and said:

—**Tengo mi color.** (*I have my color.*)

The teacher suggested:

—**Y te sientes orgullosa** (*And you feel proud.*)

—**Sí, me siento orgullosa.** (*Yes, I feel proud.*)

In another class, a shy girl sitting back in a corner, not quite in the circle, said, "I don't understand." The teacher explained and said:

Tienes tu hermanita. (*You have your baby sister.*)

Debbie quickly pulled her chair into the circle and said:

Tengo mi hermanita.

Topics for conversation are affective questions that arise naturally from each new grammar structure learned, for example:

Who are you?

What do you do all day?

What do you like to do?

What can you do well?

What bothers you? What makes you angry?

When you were a child, what did you and your friends like to do?

How did you celebrate your favorite holiday?

What did you used to wish for?

What have you done that made you feel good?

What has happened to you that made you feel bad?

What would you like to do tomorrow?

What would you do next summer if you could?

If you had only a year to live and could be successful in one thing, what would you do?

Conversation circles are not for introducing grammar but for actively using the grammar that has been learned to share personal experiences and feelings in the foreign language. We believe that grammar and pronunciation should not be corrected here because correction interrupts communication.

The teacher helps by providing a word to identify a feeling or to express what someone wants to say, maybe even writing the new words on the board or on a wall chart. When there is a need for new vocabulary to answer a question such as **"What do you like to do?"** the teacher can anticipate this by suggesting that students make drawings to illustrate their answers. While they are drawing, the teacher walks around, looks at their pictures, and gives students the words they need.

Values Clarification

We have found that meaningful use of language can take the place of most language drill through the use of values clarification strategies. Values clarification is not an attempt to teach values but rather to help young people develop a valuing process that involves:

- Choosing one's beliefs and behavior,
- Prizing and affirming them,
- Acting on them in a consistent pattern.

Interviews, rank ordering, values continuum, and incomplete sentences are strategies particularly useful in the language classroom because their linguistic content is limited enough to make it possible for even beginning language students to treat interesting, relevant, and important questions.

a. *Interviews* are one of the most useful techniques. We use three types of interviews:

- Focus interview, in which the group interviews one person;
- Group interview, in which the leader interviews all members of the group;
- Person-to-person interview, in which partners or small groups interview each other.

For all, the basic rules are the same:

- The interviewee may decline to answer any question by simply saying, "I pass";
- The interviewee may end the interview at any time by saying, "Thank you for your questions";
- The interviewee may ask any interviewer the same questions that he or she was asked.

Example of a Person-to-Person Interview

Objective: To use the verb **have.**

Everyone in the class finds a partner. The teacher first reviews the three basic rules for interviews, then interviews his or her partner as a model with questions like these:

Do you have any brothers and sisters?

Do you have a pet?

Does your family have a car?

Do you have a favorite teacher?

Does your mother have any brothers and sisters?

Do you have a favorite place?

Then each student interviews his or her partner. Afterward they return to the large group and tell something about their partners.

Example of a Group Interview

Objective: To use verbs in the present tense.

The teacher (or another leader) asks questions like the following of students at random:

Do you watch much television?

How much time do you spend watching television?

> **Do you believe that grades help you learn?**
> **Do you learn more in or out of school?**
> **Does your father buy records?**
> **Do you go to church?**
> **Do your parents go to church?**
> **How do you get money to spend?**

Example of a Focus Interview

Objective: To be able to ask questions in order to get acquainted.

The entire class regularly interviews one of its own members. To create special interest, invite a visitor from another language class or another school, a native speaker of the language, a parent, the principal, or anyone the students say they would like to interview (students can act as interpreters). The day before the visit, the class may brainstorm to prepare a list of questions to ask, or each student may prepare a list at home.

Although the teacher and students prepare interview questions ahead of time, they should feel free to think of new questions during the interview. Some interesting questions may arise during the interview.

b. *Rank ordering* gives students practice in choosing among alternatives and weighing their choices. The leader asks a question, then gives several alternative responses. Each participant lists these choices in order, according to his or her own preference. Students should always feel free to pass.

Example of Rank Ordering

Objective: To use prepositions.

Wie lernst du am besten? (*How do you learn best?*)
aus Büchern (*from books*)
vom Unterricht (*from instruction*)
durch Erfahrung (*through experience*)

The teacher responds as a model:

Ich lerne am besten aus Büchern, durch Erfahrung und vom Unterricht.

The language is simple, but the participants have to think, weigh the question against their values, and decide how to answer it.

c. The *values continuum* is a useful device to indicate the wide range of possible positions on a question. Students may use it to affirm their opinions and beliefs even when they have very little of the foreign language at their command.

Example of a Values Continuum

Objective: To understand the use of the noun form of the verb.

Where are you on this line?

Grades are necessary for learning.   Grades are not necessary for learning.

The beginning student can answer **"I am here,"** and initial a position on the line. More advanced students can initial and explain their position.

---

d. *Incomplete sentences* in any grammatical context can be used to explore attitudes, beliefs, hopes, joys, and fears.

Example of Incomplete Sentences

Objective: To understand and use the imperfect past tense.

Cuando yo era niño/a, (*When I was a child,*)

creía _____. (*I believed _____*)

quería _____. (*I wanted _____*)

esperaba _____. (*I hoped _____*)

One way to treat incomplete sentences is to write them on the board and have the students write the completed sentences in their notebooks. Then have them choose partners or form small groups and share their sentences with each other. Or the teacher might keep the whole class together and ask each person to share one sentence.

Following values clarification activities, it is appropriate and helpful to ask students to think for a minute about what they have learned, calling their attention to the following unfinished statements, which could be permanently displayed on a wall chart.

Example of "I Learned" Statements

I learned _____.	**Now I see** _____.
I realized _____.	**Now I realize** _____.
I noticed _____.	**I notice** _____.
I was surprised _____.	**I am surprised** _____.
I was pleased _____.	**I am pleased** _____.

Students are not called on to respond with these statements but may volunteer a response.

All the communication activities so far described are tightly structured. We find that limiting them in both language and content helps in the following ways:

- *Limiting grammar concepts and vocabulary to what is familiar to students* makes it possible for all of them to be involved and gives them the satisfaction of being able to perform and communicate effectively in the language.
- *Limiting communication to the sharing of thoughts and feelings without discussion* promotes respect for people's right to live, think, feel, and assign values differently.

Counseling-Learning/Community Language Learning

In contrast to the preceding activities, which are personal but controlled in linguistic content, community language learning gives students complete freedom to talk about anything they want. Stevick[1] describes the basic procedure: learners talk to each other, record what they say, listen to the recording, write it down, and identify its component parts. A small group of six to twelve students sits in a closed circle with the teacher outside the circle ready to supply the language needed. Someone in the circle initiates the conversation with a statement or question, which the teacher translates into the target language. The student repeats the sentence, at the same time recording it with a hand-held microphone. He or she turns off the microphone and hands it to someone else to respond and continue the conversation. The same procedure is followed until the conversation is concluded or the teacher calls time (five to ten minutes). This investment phase is followed by a reflection phase that involves three steps:

1. The participants talk (in their native language) about the experience in all of its aspects—cognitive, emotional, and physical. It is at this point that the exercise of reflective listening and empathy is of the utmost importance. The teacher, listening to the reactions of the learners, must show understanding and warm acceptance and must respond objectively without any show of defensiveness.
2. The learners play back the recorded conversation and listen without interruption.
3. The conversation is played again, sentence by sentence, and each sentence is translated by the person who recorded it. Then the teacher helps the students identify the component parts of the sentence and of individual words.

The procedure is simple enough, but the development of community feeling—the dynamics of working and sharing with one another on a learning task—is complex and challenging. Practitioners of counseling learning/community language learning are reluctant to talk about techniques before establishing certain basic tenets of their philosophy, namely:

- That people are whole human beings—i.e., not split between intellect and emotion or mind and body and
- That the ideal learning relationship is similar to the counselor-client interaction, with the teacher and learner alternating in the counselor-client roles according to their varying needs for being listened to with empathy.

---

1. Earl Stevick, *Memory, Meaning & Method* (Rowley, Mass.: Newbury House Publishers, 1976), pp. 125–33.

During the first stages of language learning, when students are feeling anxious because of their lack of knowledge, and somewhat later when they aggressively show their independence and indignantly resist help, the teacher must act as counselor by accepting and reflecting the feelings of the learners. At a still later stage, when students have developed some confidence in the language and some awareness of "knowing what they don't know," they, in turn, can become the "counselor" and help the teacher satisfy his or her need to impart more knowledge.

The most critical factor seems to be the attitude of teachers or resource people while they are giving information. They must be warm and friendly, without condescension or faultfinding, ready to supply information that students ask for but no more than they ask for. Stevick reports that instructors at the Foreign Service Institute in Washington, D.C., are finding community language learning "very successful linguistically and, from a psycho-dynamic point of view, quite exciting."

Although we have had some very successful experiences using this approach, we have serious doubts about its practicality in schools in which passing from level to level is based on predetermined grammar and behavioral objectives. It seems best fitted for an institute or school with student-developed objectives. Other deterrents to its practicality are large classes, grading, and the need for teachers to be well trained in counseling techniques. It is too exciting to ignore, however, and practical creative adaptations may evolve.

FORMING SMALL GROUPS

Many of the activities described in this book are done with a partner or in a small group. How do people pick partners and form groups? The answer is important to the dynamics of the class and to the total learning experience of each individual.

Think about the seating arrangement in the room. Does everyone—students and teacher— sit in the same seat every day? Is this by arrangement or by choice? If the seating arrangement does change, how and why does it change? Who initiates the change? Are partnerships and small groups always made up of the same members? Classes lack interaction and excitement when patterns continue unchanged.

To develop self-awareness and awareness of others and to establish a caring relationship among all the members of the class, we need to establish new patterns. We are generally reluctant to risk altering the pattern because we feel comfortable with the familiar. But new patterns create exciting new dynamics in the classroom, and students often welcome help in establishing them. In small-group exercises it is particularly important that students change partners from time to time.

The quickest way to form new partnerships or new groups is to count off. Decide how large you want each group to be and ask students to count off. If you want groups of three and there are twenty-one in your class, have students count off in order from one to seven, then repeat. All number ones are in one group, number twos in another, and so on.

Students may be reluctant to approach new partners and may feel awkward when asked to talk to someone they don't know very well. *Games provide another way for a class to form partnerships,* to have fun together, to get to know each other, and to learn more vocabulary at the same time. Forming new groups is valuable because it stimulates interest in communicating, develops human relations skills, and encourages peer teaching.

Usually, however, students will prefer to choose their own groups. For many activities it is preferable to let them work and share with people they already trust. It is up to the teacher to decide when to use some structured device to break up the existing patterns, when to group the students arbitrarily, and when to let them choose their own groups.

Example of Games to Form Groups

Objective: To establish new group relationships.

"People to People"

Have students pair off, with one leftover person (the teacher, the first time). The leftover person is the leader and calls out some actions for the partners to do together such as:

> **hand to hand**
> **left shoulder to left shoulder**
> **elbow to knee**

When the leader calls out **"people to people,"** all change partners, and the leftover person becomes the new leader.

After a few minutes, stop and have the class begin a new activity with the new partnerships.

Ducks and Cows (from the *New Games Book* described in the resource section at the end of the chapter)

Have the students close their eyes. The leader whispers the name of an animal in the ear of each person. (The number of different animals will depend on how many groups you want.) Tell students to make the sound of their animal and walk around with their eyes still closed until they find all the others making the same sound. Once animal groups are formed, the leader tells them to open their eyes. They are then ready to begin an activity with their new group.

REFLECTIVE LISTENING

The most valuable skill for facilitating open communication among the participants in a class or group is reflective listening, that is, showing others that you understand what they are saying and feeling. *Showing others that you understand* requires some kind of activity; it is not simply a passive state. In fact, Gordon, in training parents and teachers for greater effectiveness, calls it *active listening* and explains it in these words:

> The receiver tries to understand what it is the sender is feeling or what his message means. Then he puts his understanding into his own words (code) and feeds it back for the sender's verification. The receiver *does not* send a message of his own—such as an evaluation, opinion, advice, logic, analysis, or question. *He feeds back only what he feels the sender's message meant—* nothing more, nothing less.[2]

The listener becomes a mirror in which the speaker can see and recognize his or her own image, and correct it if the initial impression seems false.

Reflective listening unlocked the feelings of fear repressed by this sensitive girl who had always seemed poised and completely self-confident. Discovering that her feelings of fear were ac-

---

2. Thomas Gordon, *Parent Effectiveness Training* (New York: Peter H. Wyden, 1970), p. 53.

Example of Reflective Listening

Objective: To listen beyond the words.

A Spanish class at Kenston High School was going to make a trip to Mexico and live with Mexican families for three weeks. Shortly before leaving, a student came in and said,

"I can't go to Mexico; I'm sick. I've been to the doctor."

"You can't go. Because you're sick."

"Well, I'm not really sick, but that's a very scary thing."

---

cepted, she owned up to them, examined the problems, decided to make the trip, and found it a rewarding experience. This dramatic example showed us what can happen when we really listen to students. Students appreciate not being preached at or given quick advice but just listened to. We can learn a great deal about what is on their minds when we take the time to listen.

Reflective listening helps to create an environment in which teachers and students can express genuine feelings and be open to others, warmly accepting and appreciating them as individuals. In this accepting, nonjudgmental environment, people become more productive and creative, learn to solve problems, and make constructive changes. More important from a classroom standpoint, we find students less critical of each other and more willing to help each other.

> It is one of those simple but beautiful paradoxes of life: When a person feels that he is truly accepted by another, as he is, then he is freed to move from there and to begin to think about how he wants to change, how he wants to grow, how he can become different, how he might become more of what he is capable of being.[3]

Reflective listening (**"You said** _____ . **You feel** _____ .") is a systemized way of showing that you accept what people feel even if you do not approve of their actions.

REAL-LIFE EXPERIENCES

Most teachers have discovered that real-life experiences add an exciting extra dimension to foreign language study and are worth the extra effort. We find that using class meetings to decide on and arrange real-life language and cultural experiences assures student interest and involvement. Real-life experiences can include entertaining visitors in class or at home; providing services such as interpreting, tutoring, and teaching English to speakers of other languages; and, of course, field trips.

Entertaining and interviewing visitors in the classroom is simple and rewarding. It is exciting to communicate in an interesting and informative manner with native speakers of the foreign language. In the beginning, however, students may be more comfortable interviewing other students or teachers who understand their linguistic limitations.

Beginning a visit with a conversation circle, in which everyone shares some personal feeling, seems to establish good rapport with a visitor. It sets the tone for greater involvement in the interview or discussion to follow.

---

3. Ibid., p. 31.

Example of Entertaining a Visitor

Objective: To get acquainted.

A first-year Spanish class invited a Swiss exchange student to visit their class. Since Yvonne was also a beginning student of Spanish, she could join them in a conversation circle answering the question:

¿Dónde estás contenta? (*Where are you happy?*)

Having shared some personal feelings, the students then interviewed Yvonne about her home, her life here, and her feelings in school. Afterward she showed them slides with scenes of Switzerland. She appreciated the warm, friendly interest.

Students and teachers can work together to survey the community for language and cultural resources. Many cities have ethnic clubs that might send members to visit classes or might welcome student visitors to their functions. Businesses often bring in foreign visitors who may be available.

Example of Providing Services

Objective: To use language ability to help others.

1. Contact counselors, speech therapists, and special education teachers to identify children with a foreign language background who need tutoring help.
2. Contact your city's literacy council or similar organization (see the telephone directory) and churches to identify people who need help learning English. Foreign language students often have a special empathy for learners of English and can make good teachers.
3. Contact airport authorities and hospitals to offer names of students who would be willing to help non-English-speaking people.

Example of Field Trips

Objective: To experience a new—that is, foreign—environment.

1. Visit classes or share activities with another school.
2. Visit a bilingual class in an elementary school.
3. Visit a foreign language library in an ethnic neighborhood or in a university.
4. Tour an art gallery.
5. Eat the native dishes in a foreign restaurant or prepare such a meal yourselves.
6. Compare markets in different neighborhoods.

Challenge students to think of more ways to use the language and learn about the culture firsthand. Be sure, however, to prepare students well so that the experience will not be an encounter. Students need some practice in taking risks, some background knowledge of what they will see, some planning of what to look for, some sense of trust and confidence. (See Understanding Other Cultures in Chapter 3.)

Some class activities are designed especially for *developing feelings of trust.* The exciting bonus is that students are learning the language naturally without really being conscious of it.

Example of a Trust Walk

Objective: To trust someone to guide you as you walk with your eyes closed and to be aware of your own feelings.

The teacher tells the students that we communicate not only through speech but also through actions. We use our eyes, hands, and bodies to give messages. Tell them that they are going to have an experience of communicating with a partner *without talking* and, one of them, *without seeing.*

Have them find partners. Have one of each pair close his or her eyes and keep them closed while they go on a trust walk. The seeing partner will lead while the two walk together for ten minutes. Then have the partners exchange roles.

Have the students make the experience as interesting as possible by guiding their partner to touch, taste, smell, or listen to many things. Set guidelines where they can walk: the classroom, the whole building, a specified area outdoors. Tell them not to talk.

When the students return, have the partners discuss with each other, in the foreign language, these questions written on the board:

How did you feel?

Did anything scare you?

Did you prefer to lead or follow?

Did anything surprise you?

With the class in a large circle, ask who would like to complete one of the following sentences:

I felt _____ .

I learned _____ .

I was surprised _____ .

Used with these questions, the trust walk is a very effective communication activity when students have learned the past tense of verbs. The questions and sentences can be revised so that students can do this activity when they know only the present tense.

Encouraging students to be willing to risk is the focus of this exercise in identifying foods with the eyes closed.

Example of Risk Taking

Objective: To trust someone to give you foods you cannot see and to identify foods by taste alone.

Arrange a variety of foods on a table and label them in the foreign language. Give students time to look at the foods and learn their names; then have them choose partners. Have one person close her eyes, while her partner gives her different foods to taste and asks her **"Was ist das?"** (*What is that?*) After trying all the foods, have the partners reverse roles.

Afterward have the partners sit down and talk about the experience, answering these questions, which are written on the board:

Was war am schwierigsten? (*What was the hardest?*)

Was schmeckte am besten? Hättest du das erwartet? (*What tasted best? Would you have expected that?*)

Was schmeckte am schlimmsten? (*What tasted the worst?*)

Hast du etwas probiert was du mit offenen Augen nicht probiert hättest? (*Did you try anything that you would not have tried with your eyes open?*)

With activities like these, we can help students feel comfortable in the functional use of the language in real-life situations. They are acquiring grammar and vocabulary and also the very necessary confidence in their ability to relate to acquaintances and strangers.

WRITING

Our experiences and those of many other teachers show that learning to read and write go hand in hand. We begin teaching writing through dictation. Soon students can write short paragraphs patterned after models, and later they begin to write more freely on topics discussed in class. They read their papers to each other, stimulating conversation, new ideas, and then more writing, so they use the language more and more in an ever-widening spiral of thoughts, feelings, experiences, memories, hopes, and dreams.

Dictation

Students learn to write what they hear. To identify new sounds, it is helpful to use consonant and vowel charts to show how the sounds are formed with the mouth and tongue (see Reproduction Pages 55 through 58 in Appendix B). In the spelling topics of each language chapter, we introduce vowels and consonants in an order determined by their position in the mouth rather than by their position in the alphabet.

We find the following procedure for teaching sound-symbol relationships by dictation very effective:

1. Identify a sound by recalling a familiar word in which the sound occurs.
2. Write the word on the board and write the letter or letters that correspond to the sound.

3. Have individual students read the word and the letters, then think of other words with the same sound.

4. After introducing all the key words for the five or six sounds in the lesson, dictate half a dozen sentences made up of familiar words using these sounds. If you include some words whose spelling is still unfamiliar, write those on the board for students to learn as a unit rather than phonetically.

5. Have one student go to the board to write while the others write at their desks.

6. Read a sentence once at normal speed while students listen. Then repeat the sentence at the same speed and have students write it.

7. Have the student at the board read the sentence that he or she has written.

8. If there is a mistake, have the student read again *exactly* what he or she has written. When students sound out their mistakes and then repeat the original sentence, they can usually find and correct their own mistakes. If not, other students can help.

9. Have the other students correct their papers from the corrected sentences on the board.

10. Continue the dictation with different students at the board.

Words and sentences for dictation should be chosen carefully to show students the logic in the relationship between sound systems and writing systems. You can do the entire dictation procedure in the target language—including explanation of sounds and spelling rules—by providing models, demonstrating on the board, and pointing out on a mouth diagram the position of sounds in the mouth, nose, and throat. The exact procedure is described in the individual language chapters.

Composition

Once they learn the writing system, students begin to write informative paragraphs. To forestall any inclination to compose in their native language and translate into the target language, we initially provide models for students to follow.

Example of a Model Paragraph

Objective: To write a composition with limited vocabulary.

I am Ginny Wilson. I am a wife, a mother, a teacher, and a writer. I live in Fairbanks, Alaska, with my family. We live in a log house. My husband is an engineer. We like Alaska.

Sharing short written papers is a good activity for beginning a class. As soon as the first two students arrive in the classroom, they *could* start reading their papers to each other and use them as a springboard for free conversation. Both students *should* look at the same paper while its author reads it aloud. People can read their own papers better and with greater ease; in addition they may find and correct some of their mistakes. However, the primary purpose of reading the papers to each other is certainly not the correction of errors, but the sharing of thoughts, experiences, and feelings, thereby getting to know and like each other. In a mutually caring group, language learning progresses more smoothly.

Beginning compositions should be kept brief so that they may be quickly shared at the beginning of a class period and so that students are less tempted to venture beyond the limits of familiar language structure.

Writing topics generally develop quite naturally from each day's activities. The questions for conversation circles, which are based on grammar concepts under current study, make good writing topics, for example:

Who are you?

Where are you happy? Sad?

What are you going to do next summer? Next year? Some day?

As students develop linguistic skill and acquire the habits of thinking and writing without translating, their writing need no longer be structured so closely to particular grammar concepts. They begin to write creatively. For stimulating ideas and topics, we look to resources such as those described in *A Guidebook for Teaching Creative Writing* by Gene Stanford and Marie Smith in this same series.

READING

We find that students read more quickly and easily what they themselves have said or written.

When teaching beginning reading we suggest you follow these steps:

1. Demonstrate through dictation the correspondence between oral and written symbols for sounds and words.
2. Compose and write on the board a paragraph on a personal topic. Read it aloud and have students copy it as a model for compositions of their own.
3. Ask students to read their compositions aloud to a partner.
4. Encourage students to read along while their partners read aloud.

Creating Reading Material

Other sources of easily understood reading material are group compositions and transcriptions of recorded conversation.

Example of a Group Composition

Objective: To write and read an original composition.

1. Focus on a picture, a school situation, or some group experience.
2. Ask questions that elicit a story from the students.
3. Have two students act as secretaries, one to write the story on the board and one to write it on a ditto master.
4. Make copies of the story and distribute them to all the students.
5. Read the story aloud to a partner.

Example of a Transcription of a Recorded Conversation

Objective: To write dialog and read parts.

1. Help students carry on a conversation in the target language and record it.
2. Have students transcribe the recording as a group project.
3. Correct the transcription and ask a student to copy it on a ditto master.
4. Reproduce it for distribution.
5. Read it aloud, taking parts as in a play.

Using Readers

Students are soon ready for carefully graded reading selections in which new vocabulary and grammar concepts are slowly and systematically introduced. How to handle such reading material presents a problem since the content is rarely of sufficient interest or importance to justify much time spent on comprehension questions or résumés. There are several possible ways to treat such reading selections:

1. Focus on grammar analysis.
2. Use the vocabulary as a basis for personal interviews and conversation.
3. Relate themes to the lives of the students.

Example of Using a Reader

Objective: To use vocabulary to stimulate conversation and to identify grammar concepts.

Assign a story to read. The next day give students the time to ask any questions they have regarding comprehension, vocabulary, or grammar. Then have them read the story again and write five personal questions to ask other people in the class—questions suggested by the vocabulary or the situation in the story, but not about it. Have them also write their own answers.

For example, using the French basic reader **Connaître et se connaître,** students read, «**Un homme qui a tout fait, ou presque tout, dans la vie**». A student asks:

Qu'est-ce que tu as fait qui t'a rendu content? (What have you done that made you feel happy?)

Quelle est une résolution que tu aimerais réaliser? (What is a goal that you would like to achieve?)

As-tu déjà réalisé une résolution qui était difficile? (Have you already achieved some goal that was difficult?)

As-tu appris à jouer d'un instrument de musique? (Have you learned to play a musical instrument?)

Voudrais-tu apprendre à piloter un avion? (*Would you like to learn to fly a plane?*)

In class the following day, have students read the story aloud, taking turns acting out dialog parts with appropriate expression. Since the story is, by this time, quite familiar and well understood, the reading is lively. Afterwards the class divides into small groups or pairs for students to ask each other questions and continue in conversation generated by responses to the questions.

Cut the conversations short after ten or fifteen minutes, while interest is still lively. With books in hand again, identify grammar concepts. In this story, the teacher asks students to pick out uses of the past tense.

To conclude the lesson in a personal way, lead a conversation circle related to an affective theme of the story. In this instance, the teacher asks:

Est-ce qu'il y a quelque chose que tu aimerais apprendre a faire, mais que tu as peur d'essayer? (*Is there something that you would like to learn to do, but that you are afraid to try?*)

Example of Personalizing Themes

Objective: To relate themes to your own life.

1. Gather students in a semicircle by the board.
2. Brainstorm until students have suggested a number of themes from a story/poem/play.
3. Decide together which one to discuss first.
4. Discuss what was thought or felt regarding that theme by the author or a character in the story.
5. Relate the theme to the experiences of the class members with some communication strategy such as a rank-order, values continuum, or incomplete sentences.
6. Continue with one or two other themes from those listed on the board.
7. Conclude with an open-ended question, the responses shared in a conversation circle.

See Chapter 3 for more ideas on personalizing literature.

Developing Silent Reading Skills

Traditionally there has been a lot of emphasis on reading aloud in foreign language classes. Students often lose the meaning of what they read when they are preoccupied with and frustrated by the mechanics of converting letters into sounds. What we want to do in teaching reading is to develop the following skills that are needed for reading enjoyment and for information gathering:

1. Rapid reading for content,
2. Highlighting important points,
3. Identifying with the situation,
4. Recalling the gist of the material.

Here is an example of an assignment that helps develop such skills and reading strategies.

Example of a Silent Reading Assignment[4]

Objective: To read for content.

1. Read the title aloud. Encourage students to think about what it suggests to them by giving you words they associate with it.
2. Have students read the selection silently and rapidly. Set a time limit (probably 75 to 100 words a minute). Warn them a minute before the time is up so they can hurry to finish.
3. In groups of three to five students sharing a book, have them find the answers to general questions on content.
4. Working with each one individually, help students outline the reading.
   - Have them divide the text into small sections, no fewer than three.
   - Have them write a title for each section that identifies who it is, what she or he is doing, and where she or he is doing it.
   - Have them refer to each section again and list other points under the title.
5. In pairs, have the students tell the story to each other.
6. In small groups or with the whole class, ask students to talk about any similar experiences of their own.

---

4. Nicolas Ferguson and Maire O'Reilly, *English by Objectives* (London: Evans Brothers).

EVALUATION

The way teachers correct mistakes, test, and evaluate is important to students' learning and to the development of positive feelings about themselves and the class. Evaluation is a two-way street: we teachers need to be aware of mistakes we are making and the extent to which we are achieving our goals. Therefore, evaluation should be an ongoing process that is an integral part of the program.

Correcting mistakes is, of course, a necessary and important part of teaching grammar. Nevertheless, students suffer from some humiliation each time they are corrected. The tough ones who are determined to learn, shrug it off, but others feel the humiliation and become more and more silent. Realizing this, we try to limit corrections to grammar-teaching activities and avoid any other corrections except to clarify meaning. When correction is necessary, we let students help each other. If corrections are made in an accepting, nonjudgmental way, students come to be aware of the value of contrasting right and wrong and are more apt to risk making mistakes.

Correcting writing is a similar problem. Grammar exercises or tests probably require careful marking to help students understand concepts. But when students are writing compositions, it is very discouraging to get back "bleeding red" papers. Stanford and Smith[5] suggest that instead of editing entire papers and correcting them like proofreaders, we mark the kind of errors that will help students learn, diagnose mistakes, and prescribe remedies.

Class evaluation offers students and the teacher the opportunity to give each other feedback on what they see happening or being achieved in the class. It a good idea to do such evaluation in a systematic way, using some kind of instrument for self-evaluation, group evaluation, and teacher evaluation. Some quite informal evaluations are included after the various activities in the language chapters. You can find good evaluation forms in Kirschenbaum and Glaser's *Manual for Professional Support Groups* (see the resources at the end of the chapter). When the forms are completed, share the results in a class meeting. It is, of course, very important in such a meeting to be accepting and nondefensive, ending on a note of planning positive things for the future.

Testing can help motivate students and raise their self-esteem. Since it takes so long to be able to communicate in a new language, students need to feel the accomplishment of learning in small steps. We, therefore, offer suggestions for testing specific objectives at the end of each topic in the language chapters. We offer open test ideas, which invite considerable free response and personal communication. It is important to grade only the *specific language objectives* and in no way seem to judge or evaluate the communication itself.

Example of an Approach to Criteria Reference Testing

1. Test the achievement of specific objectives.
2. Make students aware of the objectives and tell them well in advance on what they will be tested.
3. Consider for grading only items that relate specifically to stated objectives.
4. Grade each student's work in relation to *his* or *her* achievement, not in comparison to other students.
5. Give students a passing grade if they have achieved at least 80 to 85 percent mastery.
6. Have students retake tests until they have achieved a passing mark.

We give short quizzes to establish mastery of grammar and vocabulary objectives. Students who do not pass must study and retake a quiz within an established time limit. We usually give tests on two consecutive days. Those students who are ready the first day take the test, while those who still have questions receive more individual attention from the teacher. The following day while the second group is taking the test, the first group is involved in other activities—reading, games, a conversation circle, making a bulletin board to introduce a new unit. There are several advantages to insisting that students retake tests until they show mastery of the objectives:

1. Students are less anxious about being tested.
2. They become more responsible for their own learning.

---

5.   Gene Stanford and Marie Smith, *A Guidebook for Teaching Composition* (Boston: Allyn and Bacon, 1977), pp. 7–16.

3. They learn how to study by using a variety of resources, such as other students, books, native speakers of the foreign language, as well as the teacher.

4. Finally, we can maintain the high standards of achievement that mark a successful language program without penalizing students.

Sometimes we involve students in determining what should be included in the test of a specific objective. When students are involved in deciding what should be tested and are actually creating sample test items, they are more likely to succeed in mastering the objectives.

A learning community in which everyone benefits is created when students are working together but still feel responsible for their own success. Thinking about testing and evaluation in this way can help open our minds to more creative possibilities.

Resources for Techniques for Teaching Communications

Here is a list of selected resources. Addresses of publishers and distributors are listed in Appendix A.

DIRECT METHOD

Materials

Cuisenaire rods. Educational Solutions. A set of colored rods, each 1 cm square, varying in length from 1 to 10 cm, devised for teaching mathematical concepts. They are attractive and intriguing to handle and talk about while learning a foreign language.

Print

Classroom Practices in Adult ESL. TESOL. A book full of suggestions for all language teachers by experienced teachers. Listed under direct method because most English language classes in this country must use some form of direct method, which is ample evidence that direct teaching in the target language does work. Of special interest is working in pairs, map work, teaching reading, and visual materials.

The Common Sense of Teaching Foreign Language by Caleb Gattegno. Paperbound. Educational Solutions, 1976. With emphasis on students' using their own linguistic powers to learn, Gattegno describes in detail techniques for using color-coded sound charts to quickly teach students to read, colored rods to set up situations for talking, and pictures to expand vocabulary and stimulate composition.

"The Silent Way," *Memory, Meaning & Method: Some Psychological Perspectives on Language Learning* by Earl W. Stevick. Paperbound. Newbury House, Publishers, 1976. A personal appraisal of teaching and observing classes learning languages using Cuisenaire rods as manipulative materials to set up learning situations. Recommended.

Teaching a Living Language edited by Ralph Hester. Hardbound. Harper & Row, 1970. Yvonne Lenard describes an approach for developing skills in oral and written composition, a "rational direct method."

AUDIOVISUAL METHOD

Equipment

GE portable tape recorder Model #3-5140A. Easily portable, works on batteries (5 C cells) or 120 volt current. Has a review switch that permits rewinding without turning it off. Use it with a hand-held mike for quick and noiseless on–off switching.

Language Master card player and recorder. Bell and Howell. Charles E. Merrill Publishing Company—distributor.

Voxcom long play card reader. Voxcom. Cassette tape recorder with a special attachment for recording and playing a strip of tape attached to a card. Excellent for easy replaying of a line that you want to repeat many times.

Print

Implementing Voix et Images de France, Part I, in American Schools and Colleges by Colette Renard and Charles Heinle. Hardbound.

Center for Curriculum Development. Heinle & Heinle Enterprises, 1969. Contains a description of the study that produced Le français fondamental, an explanation of the four teaching phases, and detailed lesson plans for teaching the French lessons. Useful not only for the French teacher but also for anyone wanting to learn the question-answer techniques for dialog presentation, grammar manipulation, and narration.

Towards a Practical Theory of Second Language Introduction by Philip D. Smith, Jr. The Center for Curriculum Development. Heinle & Heinle Enterprises, 1971. Describes a model for audiovisual lessons and concludes that this "generative" approach works so well that it challenges teachers' creativity. Students can talk, teachers have to find things for them to talk about.

"The Use of Questions to Clarify and Develop a Semantic Group," Teaching English as a Foreign Language by Nicolas Ferguson. Paperbound. Didier International, 1972. Heinle & Heinle Enterprises. Examples of questions to identify and practice structures.

COMMUNICATION STRATEGIES

"Act I," English in Three Acts by Richard A. Via. Paperbound. The University Press of Hawaii, 1976. Activities to relax, stimulate, and make aware. Describes how drama coaching techniques help students be themselves, free to express their true feelings on a moment-to-moment basis. Highly recommended.

Caring and Sharing in Foreign Language Classes by Gertrude Moskowitz. Paperbound. Newbury House, Publishers, 1978. Many ideas for real communication activities mostly patterned after values clarification. The activities are written in Spanish, French, German, and English, which makes them quick and easy to use.

"Community Language Learning," Memory, Meaning & Method: Some Psychological Perspectives on Language Learning by Earl W. Stevick. Paperbound. Newbury House, Publishers, 1976. A sensitive description of

this approach. Author values what he sees happening with students learning this way.

Counseling-Learning: A Whole-Person Model for Education by Charles A. Curran. Paperbound. C-L/CLL, 1972. Presents the intriguing idea of a class functioning as a cooperative community of listeners.

Counseling-Learning in Second Languages by Charles A. Curran. Paperback. C-L/CLL, 1976. Extensive research in relating counseling skills to the learning process, in particular to the learning of second languages through community language learning.

The First Catalogue for Humanizing Education. National Humanistic Education Center, 1978. Describes books, tapes, articles, student materials, and films. Good reference for sources.

Human Development Program by Harold Bessell and Uvaldo Palomares. Hardbound.

Human Development Training Institute, 1970. Detailed learning tasks for conversation circles. Highly recommended.

Language from Within by Beverly Galyean. Paperbound. Confluent Education Development and Research Center, 1976. Communication and awareness activities organized according to grammar objectives. In English suggested for translation. Recommended.

Personalizing Education: Values Clarification and Beyond by Leland W. Howe and Mary Martha Howe. Paperbound. Hart Publishing Company, 1974. Exciting how-to book that stresses integrating values clarification and other humanistic approaches with the total education process. It weaves theory and practice into processes that are practical and exciting for teachers to use. There are over 100 strategies and worksheets.

Real Communication in Foreign Language by Virginia Wilson and Beverly S. Wattenmaker. Paperbound. National Humanistic Education Center, 1973. Provides a variety of communication activities to build a community of trust, self-awareness, and awareness of others while mastering each new grammar objective. Exercises are oriented toward basic grammar concepts and written in such simple vocabulary and sentence forms that they are easily translated into any language.

"Review of Counseling-Learning: A Whole-Person Model for Education" by Earl W. Stevick. *Language Learning* 23 (1973): 250–71. Stevick describes the group process more clearly than Curran himself does.

Turning Points: New Developments, New Directions in Values Clarification, Vol. 1 and 2 edited by Joel Goodman. Paperbound. Creative Resources Press, 1978. Series of articles written by top humanistic educators in the field. Each volume contains a section on theory of values clarification, discussing changes and directions, applications, resources, and new strategies. Great inspiration and help to anyone interested in using values clarification strategies as a part of the curriculum.

Values and Teaching by Louis Raths, Merrill Harmin, and Sidney Simon. Paperbound. Charles E. Merrill Publishing Company, 1966. The basic text and original book on values clarification. Includes the theory, answers to many questions on classroom use, and twenty specific strategies, including chapters on the clarifying response and values sheets.

Values Clarification: A Handbook of Practical Strategies for Teachers and Students by Sidney Simon, Leland Howe, and Howard Kirschenbaum. Paperbound. Hart Publishing Company, 1972. Detailed instructions for seventy values clarification strategies with many examples for the basic strategies. Invaluable.

FORMING GROUPS

Print

The Cooperative Sports and Games Book: Challenge without Competition by Terry Orlick. Paperbound or hardbound. Pantheon Books, 1978. Exciting book that details games to play in classes or groups in which everybody cooperates and everybody wins. These games provide a positive alternative to competitive games. Well written, well illustrated, and very useful to teachers.

Developing Effective Classroom Groups by Gene Stanford. Paperbound. Hart Publishing Company, 1977. Detailed handbook to guide the teacher in applying principles of group dynamics to small-group and total-class instruction. Specific procedures and training activities are suggested for turning a collection of isolated individuals into a mature working group.

Joining Together: Group Theory and Group Skills by David W. Johnson and Frank P. Johnson. Paperbound. Prentice-Hall, 1975. Very readable presentation of the theory of groups and their value. Provides many activities to help students develop the cooperative skills needed for successful groups. Extremely useful for the teacher who wishes to understand and use groups effectively in the classroom.

The New Games Book by Andrew Fluegelman. Paperbound. Doubleday & Company, 1976. The New Games Foundation—distributor. Provides a variety of ideas for cooperative "new games." Valuable book for teachers and students for finding games easily adapted to foreign language. Games can add fun to the class, can help to create a community spirit, and are useful for getting the class to mix as well as for forming small groups.

Audio-Cassette

Developing Mature Classroom Groups by Gene Stanford. JAB Press. Forty-five minute tape that is directed at junior high and high school teachers and suggests specific ways to help students learn behaviors that form cohesive, productive groups. Very useful as a springboard for discussion in a methods class, teachers meeting, or in-service training lesson.

REFLECTIVE LISTENING

Counseling and Psychotheraphy: The Pursuit of Values by Charles A. Curran. Paperbound. C-L/CLL, 1968. Of particular use to teachers are the chapters on the art of understanding, the skilled response, and the clarification of conflicting values. Good insight into reflective listening and empathy.

Freedom to Learn by Carl Rogers. Paperbound. Charles E. Merrill Publishing Company, 1969. A basic text in humanistic education. Highly recommended.

Games People Play by Eric Berne. Paperbound. Grove Press, 1976. Every person is a composite of what has gone before, of what is happening now, and of the creative process of what will be: parent, adult, and child. States that we react in stereotyped ways according to the roles we play in each new relationship unless we become aware of what we are doing and how we can change the script. Valuable book for teachers.

I'm OK—You're OK by Thomas A. Harris. Paperbound. Harper & Row, Publishers, 1969. A valuable aid to looking at what is happening in your classroom.

Teacher Effectiveness Training by Thomas Gorden. Hardbound. Peter H. Wyden, 1973. A practical approach to problem solving in personal relationships, using active listening skills and "I-messages" (how the situation affects oneself) and looking for creative solutions acceptable to all parties. Highly recommended.

WRITING

Common Sense Composition by Isabel L. Hawley. Paperbound. Education Research Associates, 1977. Composition projects and activities to stimulate involvement. Evaluation.

Composition for Personal Growth: Values Clarification through Writing by Sidney B. Simon et al. Paperbound. Hart Publishing Company, 1973. Many activities to stimulate creative writing.

Eye Openers: A Program in Writing Awareness by David A. Sohn and Don Blegen. Paperbound Teacher's Guide. Scholastic Book Services, 1974. An exciting program created to involve students in the writing process and sharpen their skills in verbal imagery and clear communication. There is no written or oral language so the program can be used in any language. The images are varied and relevant; they are extremely well done and are guaranteed to evoke responses. Exercises suggested in the Teaching Guide range from relatively simple writing tasks to more complex assignments. Foreign language teachers could use this program to stimulate writing on all levels. The program includes a carousel tray with 93 slides, and 48 glossy photographs.

A Guidebook for Teaching Creative Writing by Gene Stanford and Marie Smith. Paperbound. Allyn and Bacon, 1977. Good ideas for stimulating students to write and for teaching them to create images, people, and events. Lists of annotated resources.

Now Poetry edited by Charles L. Cutler et al. Paper pamphlet. Xerox Education Publications, 1975. A tiny, delightful book. Recipes for writing poetry in patterns and shapes that stimulate imagination and creativity. Highly recommended because it helps us express much (ideas, concepts, and feelings) in very few words. We begin to write real poetry in a new language.

Write Now: Insights into Creative Writing by Anne Wescott Dodd. Paperback. Globe Book Company. Provides interesting activities for people to talk about and write about, creating imagery with words, exploring sensations, putting it all together in short stories, plays, and poetry. The designs for creating patterned poetry are particularly useful for learners of a new language. Simply and directly written. A must for the intermediate English language classroom library, and a valuable source book for all language teachers.

Writing Aids through the Grades by Ruth Kearney Carlson. Paperbound. Teachers College Press, 1970. Activities to inspire writing. Verse forms. Many good ideas.

READING

"Reading Is Communication, Too!" by June K. Phillips. *Foreign Language Annals* 3 (1978): 281–87. American Council on the Teaching of Foreign Languages. Reading becomes important when the materials read and the skills and strategies involved are needed for real-life situations. Includes magazine advertisements, menus, TV/radio program listings, want ads, maps, schedules, road signs, and descriptions of houses. Useful tasks to help in decoding them include listing names of things; listing descriptive words such as style, material, and size; listing action words.

The Teaching of English Used as the Language of Instruction in Secondary Education by John Wilson. Hardbound. Faber and Faber, 1967. Valuable book for all language teachers. Focuses on teaching communication—with suggestions on things to communicate—and then integrating it with grammar and phonology. Outlines steps for teaching reading of informational and literary works, relating them first to the students' experiences. Suggests a procedure for writing a group composition. Will challenge any teacher to be more creative and thorough.

"The Utility of Oral Reading in Teaching ESL," by Donald Knapp. *TESOL Newsletter,* XII, 3: 27. Strong arguments for teaching silent reading skills and using oral reading only for performance.

EVALUATION

Degrading the Grading Myths: A Primer of Alternatives to Grades and Marks edited by Sidney Simon and James Bellanca. Hardbound. Association for Supervision and Curriculum Development, 1972. Presents successful grading alternatives that can be used in elementary, secondary, and college classrooms.

"The Evaluation Session," *Developing Support Groups: A Manual for Professional Support Groups* by Howard Kirschenbaum and Barbara Glaser. Paperbound. University Associates, 1978. National Humanistic Education Center—distributor. Forms for self- and group evaluation. Design for a meeting to share information from the forms and make plans. Recommended.

Grading edited by James Bellanca. Paperbound. National Educational Association, 1977. Offers a variety of grading alternatives. Discusses disadvantages of the graded society, presents various approaches for the evaluation of students, and suggests methods for bringing about change. Includes useful sample evaluation forms.

Improving Education Assessment and an Inventory of Measures of Affective Behavior by Walcott Beatty. Paperbound. National Educational Association, 1969. Special section of well-annotated resources listing devices developed to test human behavior. Useful for teachers seeking to test human behavior development in objective terms.

Modern Language Testing: A Handbook by Rebecca M. Valette. Hardbound. Harcourt, Brace & World, 1967. Practical suggestion for classroom tests of the four skills. Descriptions of commercial texts.

Schools without Failure by William Glasser. Hardbound and paperbound. Harper & Row, Publishers, 1969. Applies Glasser's theories of reality therapy to education. Outlines programs to reduce school failure, including increased student involvement, class meetings, new grading system. A must for students and teachers.

Wad-Ja-Get?: The Grading Game in American Education by Howard Kirschenbaum, Sidney B. Simon, and Rodney W. Napier. Paperbound. Hart Publishing Company, 1971. A comprehensive summary of pros and cons, history, and research of grading and alternative grading approaches. Presented in the form of a novel about a high school undergoing grading controversy. Recommended for students and teachers.

2

Communication in English

We begin by teaching students to ask questions, thereby giving them some security and control. They can find out what they need or want to know, and they can communicate more effectively because when they ask the questions, they are more likely to understand the answers.

In this chapter we suggest specific objectives for learning the basic structure of the English language and for using that knowledge to satisfy personal needs for interaction and communication. To create a dynamic, friendly, cooperative learning environment, we suggest activities that build self-confidence and trust in others; that stimulate curiosity and that develop techniques for discovery; and that contribute to nonjudgmental, accepting attitudes.

To use these activities, look in the list below for objectives similar to those of your course of study. Refer to the topic with the same number and choose activities appropriate for your class. Activities can be adapted to complement any text materials; and, of course, they should be adapted to the cultural background, values, and interests of each class.

It is a joy to teach when you open up ways for people to discover new things, to develop their capabilities, and to make new friends.

These lessons have a bit of magic in them; they help students feel good about themselves and each other. They don't have enough magic, however, to make language learning instantaneous and painless. Students and teachers need the help of a supportive group to conquer feelings of embarrassment, doubt, and ineptness. Working in a caring group, we help assure each other successful learning experiences.

Objectives

As the result of the learning experiences in this chapter and with sufficient practice, students should be able to:

1. Introduce themselves and each other, using *subject pronouns* and the verb **be.**
2. Tell who their friends or members of their family are, using *possessive adjectives* and *singular and plural nouns.*

---

3. Write what they say, learning the *relationship between sounds and letters*.

4. Check out assumptions with *affirmative and negative questions,* using the verb **be.**

5. Describe places and the feelings those places arouse in them, using *prepositions, definite and indefinite articles,* and *adjectives.*

6. Talk about what they are doing, using the *present progressive* tense.

7. Tell what they are going to do, using the *future* tense with **going to.**

8. Talk about their families and their possessions, using *possessive pronouns* and the *possessive of nouns.*

9. Interview others about their lives, using the *simple present* tense and *adverbs* of time.

10. Tell what they like and what they like to do, using the verb **like** with *complements, nouns, object pronouns,* and *infinitives.*

11. Give directions and commands, using the *imperative.*

12. Recall past experiences, using the *simple past* tense and the auxiliary **did.**

13. Describe what they have and who gave it to them, using the verbs **have** and **give,** *direct* and *indirect objects,* and *definite* and *indefinite object pronouns.*

14. Talk about what people are like, using *adjectives with comparisons.*

15. Talk about what they will, can, should, and would like to do, using *modal auxiliary verbs.*

16. Talk about what they have done, using the *present perfect* tense.

17. Recall what happened to them that has had a lasting effect, *contrasting the present and past* tenses.

18. Speculate on what they would do under certain conditions, using the *conditional* tense.

19. Think about **look at, listen to, talk about,** and, **make sure** that they can use two- and three-word verbs.

Activities

Topic 1 "Who are you?"

> *Subject pronouns I, you, we, he, it, they; present tense of the verb be*

1.1 Sit with the class in a circle and introduce yourself.

> **I'm**   (your name).   **Who are you?**

If one person doesn't understand, go on to someone else and come back later to that one. Be relaxed and accepting so that people are not uncomfortable with mistakes.

Introduce several students saying:

This is __Jim.__ This is __Karen__ .

Who is he? Who is she?

Let students form small groups, introducing themselves and each other.

1.2 Talk about where you are from as you point to a map:

I'm in Ohio. I'm from Texas. Where are you from?

As soon as they understand, play a game. Make a ball using a wad of paper wrapped with masking tape. Everyone stand up in a circle. Pass the ball around the circle, saying:

I'm Bev.

I'm Ginny.

I'm _____ .

Call the name of someone on the other side of the circle and throw the ball to him or her. He or she calls out another person's name and throws the ball to that person. After a few throws, add some variations:

I'm from Michigan.   __Jim,__ (throw the ball to Jim) **where are you from?**

Let students continue, making up their own questions and rules.

1.3 With students in a large group, look through magazines and identify pictures:

This is a baseball player. I'm not a baseball player. Are you a baseball player?

This is a skier. Who is a skier?

Have students ask each other questions:

Who is a skier?

Are you a skier?

Who is a pianist?

Are you a tennis player?

1.4 From current magazines and newspapers, you and the students cut out pictures of well-known people in politics, government, sports, music, art, and so forth. Help students talk about them:

This is Bjorn Borg.

He is a tennis player.

He is from Sweden.

1.5 Make a collage of pictures that represent who you are, and talk about who you are. For example:

I'm Ginny Wilson. I'm a wife and a mother. I'm a teacher and also a student.

I'm a gardener.

Form small groups and give each group some magazines for everyone to make collages. Encourage them to talk about the pictures while they work.

1.6 In a conversation circle (see Chapter 1), ask:

Who are you?

After everyone has answered with several items from his or her collage, recall each other's answers:

___**Ann**___, you are a _____ and a _____ and a _____ .

___**Bob**___, you are _____ .

Encourage students to help in recalling the responses.

1.7 Test students' use of subject pronouns, the present tense of the verb **be,** and contractions. Since the subject matter is personal, take care to grade only the grammar and nativelike quality of presentation and not the content.

Oral Test Idea

Have the students introduce you to a classmate and tell you about him or her. Model:

> **This is my friend Mike. He's a football player, a baseball player, and a mechanic. My friend is a good musician, too. He's a guitar player.**

Topic 2   "Who are the others in your family?"

Possessive adjectives; singular and plural nouns

2.1 Teach the possessive adjectives, **my, your, his, her, our, their** by the direct method (see Chapter 1):

> **This is my book.**
> **Is that your book?**
> **Are these his books or her books?**

Begin lessons with just the singular form and continue later with the plural.

2.2 Have students find magazine or newspaper pictures depicting different professions and occupations, and have them learn the words for these professions and occupations:

> **This is a doctor.**
> **He is a nurse.**
> **She is a bus driver.**

Display the pictures on the wall or a bulletin board and keep them for reference in later activities.

2.3 Bring to class a photograph (or a drawing) of your family or of a group of friends, and have students do the same. Describe your own photograph. For example:

> **Here I am. This is my father. He's a shoe salesman. This is my mother. She's an accountant. This is my brother. He's in New York. This is my sister. She's a student at the university.**

Interview one person about his or her picture:

> **Where are you in the picture? Is this your father? Is this your mother? What do they do?**

Then have everyone choose a partner and talk to their partner about their picture. Afterwards, return to the large group and have each one tell about his or her partner's picture. Describe your partner's picture as a model. For example:

> **This is Mike's family. Here is his father. He's a mechanic and a fisherman.
> Here is his mother. She's a bus driver, a homemaker, and a mechanic, too.**

2.4 Test students' mastery of possessive adjectives with singular or plural nouns. Grade only the specific grammar objective.

Oral Test Idea

Prepare a half-minute talk describing your friends. Model:

> **My friends are Judy and Mike. They're tennis players. Mike's a man. Judy is
> his wife. Their son Jay is my friend too.**

Topic 3   "How do you spell . . . ?"

Correspondence between sounds and letters

3.1 Teach writing by dictation, first isolating sounds and identifying the sounds with symbols (see Chapter 1). Gesture and demonstrate so that students understand your instructions.

1. *Listen.* Have them listen to a simple sentence with a key word they understand. The ones given below are only examples.

2. *Read and spell.* Identify the sound you are teaching in the key word. Write the word on the board and spell it aloud. Have several students individually read and spell the word.

3. *Think of other words with the same sound.* Ask students to tell you other words with the same sound. Think of some words yourself; write them and read them aloud so the students understand what you want.

Dictate several simple sentences at the end of each lesson, following the practice of sounding out mistakes and correcting them (see Chapter 1, Writing). Mount on the wall a large drawing of the mouth, and each day write on it the letters taught in that lesson. To prepare the drawing, you can make a transparency from Reproduction Page 2, **"English Vowels and Consonants."** Use an overhead projector to display the enlarged image on a heavy piece of paper fastened to the wall; draw an outline of the mouth and indicate the positions in the mouth where the sounds are made.

3.2 Teach consonants as symbols to represent the sounds made by air, vocal chords, and the position of the tongue and lips. Begin with the sounds made by stopping or partially stopping the air with the lips. Have students think of words with each sound. Write the words on the blackboard and have the students read them aloud.

Labial	Listen	Read and spell	Think of other words with the same sound
voiceless stop <u>p</u>	This is my <u>p</u>en.	<u>p</u>en, p-e-n	paper, pencil . . .
voiced stop <u>b</u>	This is her <u>b</u>ook.	<u>b</u>ook, b-o-o-k	. . .
nasal <u>m</u>	He is a <u>m</u>an.	<u>m</u>an	. . .
semivowel <u>w</u>	She is a <u>w</u>oman.	<u>w</u>oman	. . .
Labiodental			
voiceless fricative <u>f</u>, also p<u>h</u>, g<u>h</u>	Two, three, <u>f</u>our. Here is a <u>ph</u>otograph. He's laug<u>h</u>ing.	<u>f</u>our, <u>ph</u>otograph, laug<u>h</u>ing	. . . . . .
voiced fricative <u>v</u>	Three, four, fi<u>v</u>e.	fi<u>v</u>e	. . .

ENGLISH VOWELS AND CONSONANTS

-v voiceless
+v voiced

nasal
air through nose

stop
air stopped by lips or tongue

affricate
air almost stopped by lips or tongue

fricative
air pushing past lips or tongue

sibilant
air through groove of tongue

lateral
air off sides of tongue

semivowel

①: only in New England, wholesome

Give students copies of Reproduction Page 3, **"Consonants (1)."** Have them work in small groups, thinking of additional words. Guide them to check the spelling in their dictionaries.

CONSONANTS (1)

The following are consonants made with the lips. Those that are underlined are voiced (vibrated in the throat).

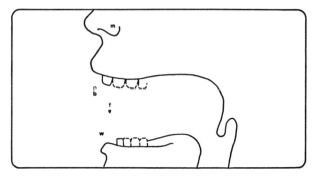

The Letter (Pronunciation)	A Word with the Letter	Other Words with the Same Sound (Perhaps Different Spelling)
m (em)	man	mom,
p (pē)	pen	pop,
b (bē)	book	ball,
f (ef)	four	photograph, laughing, five,
v (vē)	five	television,
w (dub'yōō)	woman	wall,

3.3 Teach the dental consonant **th.** If students have difficulty making the **th** sound, have them put the tip of their tongue between their teeth. Continue with the consonants formed with the tongue at the alveolar ridge just behind the upper teeth.

Dental	Listen	Read and spell	Think of other words with the same sound
voiceless fricative <u>th</u>	<u>Th</u>ank you!	<u>th</u>ank	...
voiced fricative <u>th</u>	<u>Th</u>is is my pencil.	<u>th</u>is	...
Alveolar			
voiceless stop <u>t</u>	I'm a <u>t</u>eacher.	<u>t</u>eacher	...
voiced stop <u>d</u>	This is my <u>d</u>og.	<u>d</u>og	...
nasal <u>n</u>	My mouth, my <u>n</u>ose.	<u>n</u>ose	...
lateral <u>l</u>	<u>L</u>ook at the light.	<u>l</u>ook, <u>l</u>ight	...

Give students copies of Reproduction Page 4, **"Consonants (2)."** Let them work in small groups to spell aloud the words and think of other words with the sounds.

REPRODUCTION PAGE 4

CHAPTER 2, ACTIVITY 3.3

CONSONANTS (2)

The following consonants are made with the tongue against the teeth or just behind the teeth. Those that are underlined are voiced (vibrated in the throat).

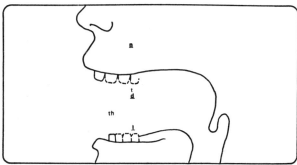

The Letter (Pronunciation)	A Word with the Letter	Other Words with the Same Sound (Perhaps Different Spelling)
n (en)	nose	nine, _____
t (tē)	teacher	ten, _____
d (dē)	dog	door, _____
l (el)	light	ball, _____
th (tē āch)	this	the, _____
(th written with two letters, but pronounced as one sound, with the tip of the tongue pushed forward between the top and bottom teeth)		_____
th (voiceless)	thanks	things, _____

3.4 Teach the consonants that are made with the tongue in the middle of the mouth. These sounds are much more difficult to distinguish from one another. The diagram showing the slightly different positions of the tongue can be helpful. Point out the spelling of **cents** and **city**. The letter **c** before **i** and **e** has the sound **s**. Most of the **z** sounds that students think of will probably be at the end of words and written with an **s**. Help them discover from their examples that the final **s** is voiced when it follows a vowel or voiced consonant, as in **is, sisters, pens**. List some familiar nouns and have them form the plurals, writing them in an /s/ column, a /z/ column, and an /ɨz/ column.

Front palatal	Listen	Read and spell	Think of other words with the same sound
voiceless sibilant **s**, also **ce, ci**	Four, five, **six**.	**six**	**cents, city** . . .
voiced sibilant **z**	Two minus two is **zero**.	**zero**	. . .
Palatal			
voiceless affricate **ch**	Here is a **chair**.	**chair**	wat**ch** . . .
voiced affricate **j**, also **g** and **-du**	I'm **jumping**.	**jumping**	**g**inger, indivi**du**al . . .
voiceless sibilant **sh**	Mike's **shirt** is blue.	**shirt**	dic**ti**onary . . .
voiced sibilant **zh**, spelled **si, su**	He u**su**ally watches televi**si**on.	u**su**ally, televi**si**on	. . .
semivowel **y**	**Yes** or no?	**y**es	. . .

Give students copies of Reproduction Page 5, **"Consonants (3)."** In small groups, have them think of other words with the same sounds. Help them discover some pattern in the spelling variations.

REPRODUCTION PAGE 5

CHAPTER 2, ACTIVITY 3.4

CONSONANTS (3)

The following consonants are made with the tongue in the middle of the mouth.
Those that are underlined are voiced (vibrated in the throat).

The Letter (Pronunciation)	A Word with the Letter	Other Words with the Same Sound (Perhaps Different Spelling)
s (es)	six	cents, city, miss,
z (zē)	zero	boys, buzz,
r (är)	red	car,
ch (sē āch) (two letters, one sound)	chair	watch,
j (jā)	jump	ginger, judge, individual, page,
sh (es āch) (two letters, one sound)	shirt	fish,
zh (zē āch) (two letters, one sound, usually spelled si, su)	Zhivago	usually, television,
y (wī)	yes	you,

3.5 Teach the consonants made with the tongue at the back of the mouth. Point out that **c** has the sound of **k** except before **e, i, y.** Point out that **ng** usually represents one nasal sound. Have students notice the difference between **sing-er** and **fin-ger** and **gin-ger.**

Velar	Listen	Read and spell	Think of other words with the same sound.
voiceless stop k, also c, q, /ks/ spelled x	Fifty kilometers.	kilometers	black . . .
voiced stop g, /gz/ spelled x	The pie is good.	good	leg, exam . . .
nasal ng	She's singing.	singing	. . .
Glottal voiced fricative h	She's going home.	home	. . .

Give students copies of Reproduction Page 6, **"Consonants (4)"** and have them work in small groups to spell and write other words.

CONSONANTS (4)

The following consonants are made at the back of the mouth and in the throat.
Those that are underlined are voiced (vibrated in the throat).

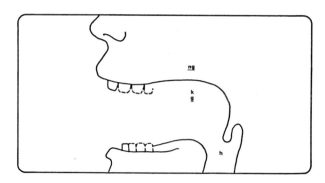

The Letter (Pronunciation)	A Word with the Letter	Other Words with the Same Sound (Perhaps Different Spelling)
ng (en jē) (one sound, two letters)	song	singing,
k (kā)	kilometer	cat, cute, coat, black, queen,
g (jē)	good	exam, leg,
h (āch)	home	help,

3.6 English vowels are difficult to spell because there are sixteen vowel sounds to represent with only five or six letters. The vowels are quite different from those of most other languages. They consist of about nine short sounds, which tend to be so relaxed that they are difficult to distinguish one from another, and seven glides and diphthongs.

Give students copies of Reproduction Page 7, **"Vowels (1)."** Identify the vowels in sentences and words. Then have students think of other words with the same sounds. Write them on the board and have students read them aloud.

VOWELS (1)

Short vowel sounds in English are different from vowels in most other languages.
They are generally more relaxed.

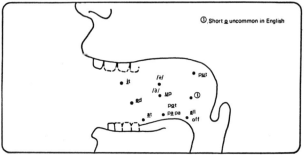

Tongue forward, lips spread	Other Words with the Same Sound
⤳ it	sit, is, _____
⤳ edge	red, pencil, _____
⤳ at	cat, black, _____
Tongue back, lips rounded	
⊙ put	book, full, _____
⊙ off	all, on, _____
Tongue middle, lips open and round	
◯ papa, pot	top, mama, _____
⊙ up	butter, cup, _____
Tongue and lips relaxed in unstressed syllables	
lion	orange, middle, _____
(after vowels and voiced consonants)	
city	bicycle, _____
(after voiceless consonants)	

3.7 It is interesting to have students notice that what are often described as long vowels in English are actually diphthongs or glides made by moving from short vowel positions toward Latin **i** and **u** sounds. Give students copies of Reproduction Page 8, **"Vowels (2)."** Help them identify the sounds and think of, write, and read other words.

REPRODUCTION PAGE 8

CHAPTER 2, ACTIVITY 3.7

VOWELS (2)

Longer vowels are actually diphthongs or glides made by the movement of the tongue and lips from one vowel position toward another.

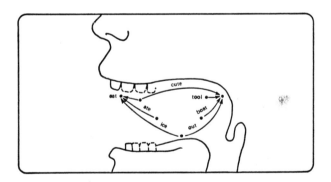

Longer Vowels Glides	Letter	Other Words with the Same Sound
eat	e	please, green, _____
ate	a	name, table, _____
ice	i	pie, like, _____
out	ou	house, brown _____
boat	o	close, window, _____
tool	oo	school, blue, _____
cute	u	united, few, you, _____

3.8 Test students' mastery of spelling and writing.

Oral and Written Test Idea

Have each student spell his or her name while another student writes it down. As a model, go to the board and ask a student:

> **What is your full name?**
>
> **Spell your first name, please.**
>
> **How do you spell your last name?**

Write the name on the board letter by letter as the student spells it. Then have that student go to the board and ask another student the same thing. Continue until all have participated.

Topic 4 "Aren't you?" "Isn't he?"

> *Affirmative and negative statements, questions with the verb* **be,**
> *and tag questions and short answers* . · ˙

4.1 Even though you and the students have been using questions and negative statements to some extent, it is helpful to contrast them in a graphic way.

Draw on the board or wall chart a diagram like the one below. We think coloring the slots helps make the sentence pattern more easily understood. For example, coloring the **be** verb slot red emphasizes the fact that the verb changes position.

	(red)	*(blue)*	*(red)*	*(yellow)*	*(green)*
Yes *Statement*		**He**'s **He**	**is**		**a student** **a student.**
Question	**Is** **Isn't**	**he** **he**			**a student?** **a student?**
No *Statement*		**He** **He**'s **He**	**is** **isn**'t	**not** **not**	**a student.** **a student.** **a student.**

Erase the word **student** and let the students help you think of other appropriate words to write in that space:

> **baseball player**
>
> **swimmer**
>
> **reader**

Give them copies of Reproduction Pages 9 and 10, **"The Verb Be in Questions and Answers,"** and have them color code their worksheets as you have done in your diagram.

With the class paired or arranged in small groups, fill in the blank spaces. With beginning students you may want to make one lesson with just third person forms, using Reproduction Page 9, and plan another lesson with the first and second person forms on Reproduction Page 10. If students are very proficient, you may prefer to let them work out all the personal subject pronouns at the same time.

REPRODUCTION PAGE 9

CHAPTER 2, ACTIVITY 4.1

THE VERB BE IN QUESTIONS AND ANSWERS (1)

Fill in all the blank spaces.

3rd person singular, masculine

	(red)	(blue)	(red)	(yellow)	(green)
Yes		He	's		a
		He	is		a
?	Is	he			a
	Isn't	he			a
No		He	is	not	a
		He	's	not	a
		He	is	n't	a

3rd person singular, feminine

	(red)	(blue)	(red)	(yellow)	(green)
Yes		She	's		a
?					
No					

3rd person plural

	(red)	(blue)	(red)	(yellow)	(green)
Yes		They	're		students.
		They	are		
?					
No					

Who?

	(red)	(blue)	(red)	(yellow)	(green)
Yes?		Who	's		a
No?					

REPRODUCTION PAGE 10

CHAPTER 2, ACTIVITY 4.1

THE VERB BE IN QUESTIONS AND ANSWERS (2)

Fill in all the blank spaces.

2nd person singular

	(red)	(blue)	(red)	(yellow)	(green)
Yes		You	're		a
		You	are		a
?	Are	you			a
	Aren't	you			a
No		You	are	not	a
		You	're	not	a
		You	are	n't	a

2nd person plural

	(red)	(blue)	(red)	(yellow)	(green)
Yes		You	're		students.
?					
No					

1st person plural

Yes		We	're		students.
?					
No					

1st person singular

Yes		I	'm		a student.
?					
	Am	I		not	a student?
No					

4.2 Prepare a stack of cards that can fit in the subject slot of the diagrams (use students' names; the personal pronouns, **I, you,** and so on; and other subjects). Then prepare cards with forms of **be** and white cards with **not** and **n't.** Prepare a stack of cards with the predicate, using singular nouns with **a** or **an,** and plural nouns with no article. Form small groups. Give each group stacks of cards of each color and ask them to form five or six sentences while you go from group to group, checking their sentences. (If you color the slots and use colored paper or pen to match, it will make the lesson more graphic.)

4.3 Use colored rods or other objects to set up visual models of families for students to use in interviewing each other.

Pick up different colored rods to represent people in your family (or a group of friends if family does not seem an appropriate topic for your class discussion). Place the rods, one by one, on the table in front of you, describing whom they represent:

Here I am. I am a teacher. This is my brother Bob.

This is my brother Frank. This is my sister Anne, and here is my sister Jean.

Let the students set up models of their own families. When they talk about them, encourage other students to ask them questions:

Is your brother a soccer player?

Isn't he a student?

Isn't your sister an artist?

Is she a swimmer?

To help students think of questions, point to pictures you have on the walls showing various professions and hobbies. Guide the students to respond with short answers

Yes, he is.

No, he's not.

No, he isn't.

Yes, she is.

No, she's not.

No, she isn't.

Yes, they are.

No, they're not.

No, they aren't.

4.4 Help the students write brief compositions about themselves and the people they have been talking about. Write a model composition that they can copy very closely. The first time, they should have to change only a few words to make it their story, for example:

> **I am Ginny Wilson. My brother Bob is an engineer. He is also a sailor. My brother Frank is a farmer. He is also a hunter and a fisherman. My sister Anne is a teacher. My sister Jean is a musician. They are also homemakers and good gardeners.**

As students finish their compositions, have them choose a partner and sit together to read aloud and listen to each other's composition. Have them sit side by side so that both of them can see the paper. If they want to, they ask questions or talk about what they have read. Then the other person reads his or her paper aloud. Afterward, all change partners and share the papers one more time.

4.5 In a large group, let each participant share something that she or he has learned about someone else in the group. Listen carefully and encourage students to make sure that everyone is remembered. Share some things you have learned as well.

4.6 Use some of the general, not-too-personal, information learned in the preceding activities to make relevant statements with short tag questions, such as "Isn't she? Is he?" to check if your statement is true.

> **__Cristina__ is an artist, isn't she?**
>
> **Yes, she is. / No, she's not. / No, she isn't.**
>
> **__Bob__ isn't a basketball player, is he?**
>
> **Yes, he is. / No, he's not. / No, he isn't.**

Point to your pictures representing professions and hobbies to remind students what to say, and have them make affirmative and negative statements with tag questions and short answers. After a few minutes of confirming or denying third person singular statements, change to plural:

> **__Sam__ and __Ted__ are tennis players, aren't they?**
>
> **They aren't singers, are they?**

Later, introduce questions for the second person:

> **__Heidi__ , you're a swimmer, aren't you?**
>
> **You aren't a skier, are you?**
>
> **__Gretchen__ and __Glen__ , you're swimmers, aren't you?**
>
> **You're not skiers, are you?**

4.7 Have students refer to Reproduction Pages 9 and 10 in Activity 4.1 and pick out the phrases that can be used as tag questions. Draw a circle around each affirmative and negative pair:

is he	**is she**	**are they**
isn't he	**isn't she**	**aren't they**
are you	**are we**	**am I**
aren't you	**aren't we**	**am I not**

Choose partners and sit together in pairs, using tag questions to check out some statements about each other:

> __Jeff__ , you're a tennis player, aren't you?
>
> **No, I'm not.**
>
> **You're a skier, aren't you?**
>
> **Yes, I am.**
>
> **You're not a golfer, are you?**
>
> **No, I'm not.**

4.8 With students together in a large group, each of you think of an affirmative and a negative statement about yourself and about one other person:

> **I'm a swimmer, but I'm not a tennis player.**
>
> __Karen__ **is a skier, but she's not a tennis player.**

Then that person makes a statement about himself or herself and about someone else. Continue until everyone has had a turn.

4.9 Test students' use of affirmative and negative questions and tag questions.

Oral and Written Test Idea

Make up ten affirmative or negative statements and ask tag questions to verify them. Example:

> **The president isn't from Florida, is he?**
>
> **Washington, D.C. is the capital, isn't it?**

After writing your questions, ask them of someone in the class.

Topic 5   "Where are you?" "How are you?"

Prepositions; definite and indefinite articles; adjectives

5.1 Teach the indefinite article **a,** the definite article **the,** and prepositions, using Cuisenaire rods and the Silent Way described in Chapter 1 (or simply use different colored pencils or paper).

> **This is a blue rod and this is a red one.**
>
> **The blue rod is on top of the red one.**

5.2 Use the colored rods to lay out a floor plan of your room, or draw one.

> **These are the walls. This is the door. Those are the windows. The bed is next to the window. The lamp is on the table next to the bed. The radio is next to the lamp.**

Let the students lay out their own rooms and talk about them.

5.3 To help students write compositions describing their rooms, give them a copy of Reproduction Page 11.

5.4 Practice the use of **a** and **the** and prepositions in a game of finding things. On a table, place a number of common classroom or personal articles: book, pencil, pen, comb, knife. Identify each item:

> *Teacher:* **What is this?**
>
> *Student:* **It's a _____ .**

REPRODUCTION PAGE 11

CHAPTER 2, ACTIVITY 5.3

MY ROOM

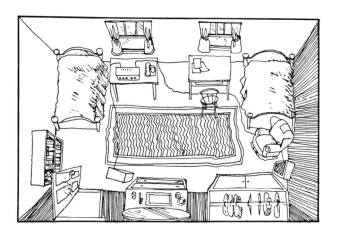

In my room there are two beds. There is a window at the head of each bed. There is a rug on the floor. The desk and chair are between the two beds. The bookcase is at the foot of my bed. The telephone and the stereo are on the table beside the bed. The dresser is near the door next to the closet, and the two speakers are on the floor. It's a nice room!

Let students help each other learn the names of all the things. Then tell the students to close their eyes while you hide one of the items. When they open their eyes, ask:

Teacher: **What is missing? What is not on the table?**

Student: **The _____ is not on the table.**

Teacher: **Ask me where it is.**

Student: **Where is the _____ ?**

Teacher: **It's under the wastebasket.**
It's behind the door.
It's on top of the cupboard.

The students then go and get the item.

After the students learn the prepositions, change the format of the game so that one of the students hides the item, and the teacher and the other students take their turns by playing twenty questions to locate it:

Is it under the teacher's desk?

No, it's not.

As soon as the students understand the format of the game, divide the class into small groups to continue the game on their own. The teacher can monitor the activity and be aware of any need for help. Make it fast and fun.

5.5 Try a variation on this game. Have students get partners; one of them thinks of an object in the room, describes it, and tells where it is; the partner guesses what it is:

> **It's white and blue. It's on the wall. It's above the wastebasket. What is it?**
>
> **It's the map.**

5.6 How are you today? Make a continuum. Have students place their initials at a spot that matches their feelings.

| excited | happy | fine | okay | tired | sick | sad | angry |

5.7 Have small groups respond to some rank-order questions (see Chapter 1). First have students walk around for two minutes, greeting each other in English, and then have them form groups of four. Announce the questions to all the groups scattered around the room and wait while the four members of each group give their answers to each other. Then continue with the next question:

> **When are you excited?**
> **on a trip**
> **at a party**
> **at a football game**

Give your answer in order of preference.

> **When are you bored?**
> **at home**
> **at a store**
> **in the classroom**
>
> **Where are you nervous?**
> **in an exam**
> **at the dentist**
> **on a plane**
>
> **Where are you contented?**
> **at the dinner table**
> **at the beach**
> **in the woods**

5.8 Make a list of places where people are during the course of a week. Make simple drawings on the board and label them. For example:

> **in a car**
> **in the classroom**
> **at home**
> **in bed**
> **at the table**
> **in the grocery store**
> **in the woods**
> **at the beach**
> **on my motorcycle**

Elicit suggestions from the students; encourage them to come to the board and illustrate places they want you to help them name. Or provide magazines from which they can choose pictures of places.

Have students help you make a list of feelings. You or they can draw faces to illustrate the feelings, or (better yet) act out the feelings yourselves. Then give students Reproduction Page 12, **"Places and Feelings,"** and have them complete the sentences, describing where they are and how they feel.

Example:

> **When I'm at the beach, I'm contented.**
>
> **When my father is at the store, he's bored.**

PLACES AND FEELINGS

Think of places where you are during a typical week and how you feel there. Complete the following sentences.

1. When I'm _____ at school _____ , I'm happy.
   When ___ Tom ___ is ___ at a basketball game, he's happy.

2. When I'm _____, I'm excited.
   When _____ is _____.

3. When I'm _____, I'm contented.
   When _____ is _____.

4. When I'm _____, I'm sad.
   When _____ is _____ .

5. When I'm _____, I'm nervous.
   When _____ is _____.

6. When I'm _____, I'm bored.
   When _____ is _____.

7. When I'm _____, I'm _____.
   When _____ is _____.

8. When I'm _____, I'm _____.
   When _____ is _____.

5.9 Test students' use of prepositions, definite and indefinite articles, and adjectives.

Oral Test Idea

Prepare a half-minute talk on where people and things are in the classroom.

Written Test Idea

> **What is on the teacher's desk?**
>
> **What is in the cabinet?**
>
> **What is outside the window?**

Topic 6 **"What are you doing?"**

Verbs in the present continuous tense (present progressive)

6.1 Gather students in a circle and demonstrate various activities, such as walking, running, and jumping (or quieter ones, such as reading, writing, drawing). Then tell students to perform the activities and ask what they are doing. For example:

> **I'm walking.   Ann   , walk around the circle!** (Gesture.)
>
> **I'm running.   Bob   , run around the circle!**
>
> **I'm jumping.   Cathy   , jump up and down!**
>
> **Who is walking?** (Imitate walking with your fingers.)
>
> **Who is running?**
>
> **Who is jumping?**

To make room for activities in a large class, sit with a group in a small circle and have the other students in a larger circle around the small circle. Have students in the outer circle perform an activity such as walking, running, or jumping. Have the students in the inner circle talk about the activities being performed.

6.2 Add a light-hearted touch with a song. Longman's has a cassette with some "grammar" songs. The music is good, the songs are really fun, and good teaching too. Try "Present Continuous Baby" with audiovisual teaching techniques.

    Here are the words and some drawings to illustrate meaning (see Reproduction Page 13, **"Present Continuous Baby"**).

REPRODUCTION PAGE 13

CHAPTER 2, ACTIVITY 6.2

PRESENT CONTINUOUS BABY

I'm walking down the street; I'm waiting for a bus.

I'm watching an old lady who's holding a small dog.

I'm looking in the windows of the shops along the way.

I'm thinking of my true love, who's the angel of the day.

I can't see her in the city of light.

I can't hear her in the dark of the night.

Make a transparency of Reproduction Page 13. Project it so that the whole class can easily see the illustrations. To play the song, use a cassette player with a quick review button and a pause control or handheld on-off switch. Play the song through once, pointing to the appropriate pictures to help students understand. Rewind to the first line and repeat it, following the procedure described in Chapter 1, Audiovisual Method.

1. Play the tape:

I'm walking down the street; I'm waiting for a bus.

Teacher		Student
What's this? (Point to the street.)	tape	**It's a street.**
What's he doing?	tape	**He's walking down the street.**
What's this? (Point to the bus.)	tape	**It's a bus.**
What's he doing?	tape	**He's waiting.**
You are the man, what are you doing?	tape	**I'm walking down the street. I'm waiting for a bus.**

Have several students repeat the line and finally let everyone sing along.

2. Play the tape:

I'm watching an old lady who's holding a small dog.

Teacher		Student
Who is this? (Point to the lady.)	tape	**She's a lady.**
Is she an old lady or a young lady?	tape	**She's an old lady.**
What is this? (Point to the dog.)	tape	**It's a dog.**
Is it a big dog or a small dog?	tape	**It's a small dog.**
What is the lady doing?	tape	**She's holding a small dog.**
What is the man doing?	tape	**He's watching.**
Who's holding the dog?	tape	**An old lady.**
You are the man, what are you doing?	tape	**I'm watching an old lady who's holding a small dog.**

3. Play the tape:

I'm looking in the windows of the shops along the way.

Teacher		Student
What are these? (Point to the shops.)	tape	**They're shops.**
What is this? (Point to a shop.)	tape	**It's a shop.**
What are these? (Point to the windows.)	tape	**They're windows.**
What is this? (Point to a window.)	tape	**It's a window.**
What windows are they?	tape	**They are the windows of the shops.**
Where are the shops?	tape	**They're along the way.**
What is the man doing?	tape	**He's looking in the windows.**
You are the man, what are you doing?	tape	**I'm looking in the windows of the shops along the way.**

4. Play the tape:

I'm thinking of my true love, who's the angel of the day.

Teacher		Student
Is it day or night? (Point to the sun.)	tape	**It's day.**
What is this? (Point to the angel.)	tape	**It's an angel.**
What is the man doing? (Point to his head.)	tape	**He's thinking.**
Who is he thinking of?	tape	**He's thinking about his true love.**
You are the man, what are you doing?	tape	**I'm thinking of my true love, who's the angel of the day.**

5. Play the tape:

I can't see her in the city of light.

Teacher		Student
What is this? (Point to the city.)	tape	**It's a city.**
Is it light or dark?	tape	**It's light.**
Can he see his true love?	tape	**No, he can't see her.**
Where can't he see her?	tape	**He can't see her in the city of light.**
You are the man, can you see her?	tape	**No, I can't see her in the city of light.**

6. Play the tape:

I can't hear her in the dark of night.

Teacher		Student
Is it day or night?	tape	It's night.
Is it light or dark?	tape	It's dark.
Can he hear her?	tape	No, he can't hear her.
You are the man, can you hear your true love?	tape	I can't hear her in the dark of the night.

This song is recorded in England. It's interesting to point out some differences in pronunciation. Notice the broad **a** in the last two lines. Show students on the vowel chart, Reproduction Page 7, the position of the American **a** in **can't** and the British **a** farther back.

6.3 Using the vocabulary from the song "Present Continuous Baby," help students to talk about what they like doing. Give the students copies of Reproduction Page 14, **"What Are You Doing?"** After the students have put their activities in order of preference, ask them to share their most preferred activity with the whole class.

REPRODUCTION PAGE 14

CHAPTER 2, ACTIVITY 6.3

WHAT ARE YOU DOING?

Fill in the missing word.

I'm _____ through the woods.

I'm _____ television.

I'm _____ on a stool.

I'm _____ by a lamppost.

I'm _____ a small dog.

I'm _____ a magazine.

Copy these sentences in the order of your preference of the activity involved.

1. _____
2. _____
3. _____
4. _____
5. _____
6. _____

6.4 Have students draw pictures of what they are doing when they are either happy, sad, or excited. Have them work in small groups, asking each other questions. For example:

Where are you?

What are you doing?

How are you?

Draw a picture of yourself (just a stick figure in a rough sketch) and have them ask you the questions. Conclude by pointing to the picture and saying something like:

I'm happy reading in my living room.

Write your caption under your picture and help students write theirs.

6.5 Gather a group of no more than twelve students in a conversation circle (see Chapter 1). Have them bring their pictures from activity 6.4. Say:

Tell us about your picture, what you are doing, how you feel while doing it, and where you are doing it.

Participate with the students; present your reply as a model.

I'm happy hiking in the mountains.

After everyone has taken a turn or passed, recall what each has said, speaking directly to that person.

___Doug___ , you are excited water-skiing on the lake.

___Barry___ , you are happy swimming in the pool.

Encourage students to continue recalling each other's responses.

6.6 Review the verb **be** in the singular and plural. Give the students copies of Reproduction Page 15, "Who Are You?"

REPRODUCTION PAGE 15

CHAPTER 2, ACTIVITY 6.6

WHO ARE YOU?

1. Who are you?

   I'm a   We're

   I'm not a   We're not

2. Where are you?

   I'm   We're

   I'm not   We're not

3. What are you doing?

   I'm   We're

   I'm not   We're not

4. How are you?

   I'm   We're

   I'm not   We're not

6.7 Test students' use of the present continuous tense.

Written Test Idea

1. _____ is _____ .
2. I'm _____ .
3. He' _____ _____ .
4. They _____ _____ .
5. _____ and I _____ _____ .
6. _____ and _____ _____ _____ .
7. They' _____ _____ .
8. She' _____ _____ .
9. Mr. _____ _____ _____ .
10. Ms. _____ _____ _____ .

Oral Test Idea

Have students demonstrate to the class how to do something (eat a bag of popcorn, read a book, ride a motorcycle, ski), without talking. Either videotape the demonstration or have the student make sketches of what he or she is doing at each step. Afterwards have the class look at the videotape replay (or the pictures) while the student tells what he or she is doing step by step.

Topic 7   "What are you going to do?"

Future with going to plus the infinitive

7.1 Provide students with the following model:

> **I'm going to walk. Am I walking?**
>
> **No. I'm going to walk.**

Then walk and say:

> **Am I walking now?**
>
> **___Ellen___, run!** (Stop her with your hand.) **Wait!**
>
> **Are you running? Are you going to run?**
>
> **What is ___Ellen___ going to do?**

Continue with other action verbs.

7.2 Interview a student about his or her plans for the next day (see Chapter 1, Public Interview). Afterwards, form groups of three and interview each other:

> **What are you going to do tomorrow?**
>
> **What are the most important things you are going to do?**
>
> **What is the most boring thing you are going to do?**

7.3 In a conversation circle (see Chapter 1), ask:

> **What is the most interesting thing that you are going to do next summer?**

Recall students' answers:

> **___Koko___, you are going to travel.**

7.4 Give each student a copy of Reproduction Page 16, **"An Imaginary Trip."** Tell each student to plan a dream trip. In groups of three, tell one student to describe his or her trip while the other two listen. When the speaker finishes, the other two tell the speaker everything they remember about the trip. Continue until all have had a turn. End the activity with each group sharing a few highlights with the whole class.

AN IMAGINARY TRIP

Describe your imaginary trip to a small group of classmates.

1. Where are you going to go?

2. How are you going to go?

3. When are you going to go?

4. With whom are you going to go?

5. How long are you going to stay?

6. What are you going to do there?

7. Where are you going to live?

8. Are you going to work?

9. Are you going to have a lot of free time?

10. Are you going to read a lot?

11. What are you going to take with you?

12. Are you going to buy a lot of new things for the trip?

13. What are you going to miss at school?

14. To whom are you going to write?

15. Who is going to miss you?

16. Whom are you going to miss?

7.5 In a conversation circle, ask:

> **What are you going to do someday?**

7.6 Test students' ability to talk about the future with **going to.**

Oral Test Idea

Prepare a half-minute to one-minute sketch about someone in the class, predicting that person's life based on what you know about him or her. Draw names (including the teacher's) until every class member is chosen. Keep the names secret. After each student finishes the speech, the class can guess who was described. Model:

> **He is going to graduate from the University of Colorado. He is going to live in a geodesic dome in the mountains. He is going to ski in the winter, and he is going to go rock climbing in the summer. He is going to earn a living building furniture. He's going to be very happy. Who is he?**

Written Test Idea

1. Make a list of ten things you are going to do next summer.
2. What is the most interesting thing you are going to do?
3. What is the most boring thing you are going to do?
4. What is the most important thing you are going to do?
5. Are you going to change during the summer?
6. What are you going to learn?

Topic 8 "Whose is it?"

Possessive of nouns; possessive pronouns mine, yours, his, hers,
  ours, theirs

8.1 Teach the possessive of nouns with objects. Identify pencils, pens, colored rods:

  Which one is Koko's pencil?

  Which one is Karen's pen?

  Which one is Jeff's colored rod?

Afterwards, show them the formation of the possessive. On the board, write students' names plus a possession of theirs. For example:

  Margaret's dress

  Karen's blouse

  Chris's shirt

Get students to read them and rewrite them in columns of voiced, voiceless, and /ɪz/ endings, noting the final sounds of the names.

  Whose is this?
  Whose shirt is this?

8.2 Play a game with possessives.

  I see something blue (red, green).

  It's not Bill's shirt. (Touch Bill's shirt, shaking your head negatively.)

  It's not Mary's dress. What is it?

Encourage students to get up and point at objects and let you give them the words they need to ask the questions.

  Is it Susan's blouse?
  Is it the map?

As soon as the students get the idea for the game, let them play in small groups while you help provide words. Have students follow this pattern:

  I see something.
  What color is it?
  It's blue .

Is it   Fernando's   shirt?

No, it's not.

Is it _____ .

8.3 Talk about family relationships using **"A Family Tree,"** Reproduction Page 17.

A FAMILY TREE

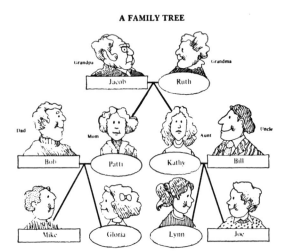

Gloria is Mike's sister. He is her brother.

She is Bob's and Patti's daughter. They are her parents.

Gloria is Ruth's and Jacob's granddaughter. They are her grandparents.

She is Kathy's and Bill's niece. They are her aunt and uncle.

She is Lynn's and Joe's cousin. They are her cousins.

Draw your own family tree. Describe it like this:

I am   Gloria   .

I am   Mike's   sister. He is my brother.

I am . . . .
Continue!

8.4 Teach the possessive pronouns. Have everyone take out items from their pockets or purses.

Model:

These keys are mine.

Those are yours.

Which ones are   Sam's   ? Those are his.

Are those   Mary's   ? Yes, they are hers.

These are ours.

Those are theirs.

Encourage each student to use similar phrases to talk about their possessions.

8.5 Pass a bag and have everyone put some possession (a ring, a pencil, a ribbon) into it without the others seeing the item. One person begins by taking an item out of the bag and trying to guess whose it is.

__Jill__ , is this __ribbon__ yours?

Yes, it's mine. / No, it's not mine.

If the ribbon is Jill's, she takes it and continues the game by pulling another item from the bag. If the guess is incorrect, the person puts the item back in the bag, takes out another one, and guesses again:

__Betty__ , is this yours?

8.6 Test students' use of possessive nouns and pronouns.

Written Test Idea

Model:

> **This book is Ken's. It is his.**
> **The desk is the teacher's. It is hers.**

The red pen is _____ .	It is _____ .
The chairs are _____ .	They are _____ .
The desk is _____ .	It is _____ .
The pencils are _____ .	They are _____ .
The white blouse is _____ .	It is _____ .
The blue jeans are _____ .	They are _____ .

Oral Test Idea

Have students describe things they see in the room by using the above pattern.

Topic 9 "Where do you live?" "What do you do?"

Verbs in the simple present tense; adverbs of time

9.1 Using the direct method (see Chapter 1) teach the simple present of several verbs that are useful in interviewing and getting acquainted.

Teacher: **I live in Fairbanks, Alaska. Where do you live, __Ann__ ?**

Student: **I live in Chagrin Falls, Ohio.**

Teacher: **Where do you live, __Bob__ ?**

Student: **I live in Tanglewood.**

Teacher: **__Ann__ lives in Chagrin Falls, Ohio. Where does __Bob__ live?**

Student: **__Bob__ lives in Tanglewood.**

Teacher: **__Cindy__ , ask __Don__ where he lives.**

Student: **__Don__ , where do you live?**

Student: **I live in Chagrin Falls.**

Teacher: **__Don__ , you live in Chagrin Falls. Where do I live?**

Student: **You live in Fairbanks, Alaska.**

Teacher: **I go to the University of Alaska. Where do you go to school, __Ann__ ?**

Student: **I go to Kenston High School.**

Teacher: __Bob__ **, where does __Ann__ go to school?**

Student: **She goes to Kenston High School.**

You may want to stop at this point and ask:

How does __Bob__ know to answer, "She goes ..."?

We trust him to think it through, but if Bob doesn't figure it out, someone else will, and can help him answer.

9.2 Teach students to use the auxiliary verb **do** in order to ask and answer affirmative and negative questions.

On a wall chart, draw a diagram like the one below. Color slots as suggested in Activity 4.1.

	(red)	*(blue)*	*(red)*	*(yellow)*	*(orange)*
Yes Statement		**He**			**works.**
Question	**Does**	**he**			**work?**
	Doesn't	**he**			**work?**
No Statement		**He**	**does**	**not**	**work.**
		He	**does**	**n't**	**work.**

Erase the verb **work** and let the students write other verbs or phrases in that space.

Give the students copies of Reproduction Pages 18 and 19, **"The Auxiliary Verb Do,"** and have them color code the slots as in your diagram. Working with partners or in small groups, fill in the blank spaces, using different verbs or phrases to complete the sentences.

REPRODUCTION PAGE 18

CHAPTER 2, ACTIVITY 9.2

THE AUXILIARY VERB "DO"

Fill in the blank spaces.

3rd person singular, masculine

	(red)	*(blue)*	*(red)*	*(yellow)*	*(orange)*
Yes		He			works.
?	Does	he			work?
	Doesn't	he			work?
No		He	does	not	work.
		He	does	n't	work.

3rd person singular, feminine

	(red)	*(blue)*	*(red)*	*(yellow)*	*(orange)*
Yes		She			works.
?					
No					

3rd person plural

Yes	::::::::::	They	::::::::::	::::::::::	work.
	Do		::::::::::	::::::::::	
?	Don't		::::::::::	::::::::::	
No	::::::::::				

Add a tag question to each *Yes* or *No* statement above and answer it with a short sentence. **Example:**

He works, doesn't he?
Yes, he does./ No, he doesn't.

He doesn't work, does he?
Yes, he does./ No, he doesn't.

REPRODUCTION PAGE 19

CHAPTER 2, ACTIVITY 9.2

THE AUXILIARY VERB "DO"

Fill in all the blank spaces.

2nd person singular or plural

	(red)	(blue)	(red)	(yellow)	(orange)
Yes	::::::::::	You	::::::::::	::::::::::	work.
?			::::::::::	::::::::::	
No	::::::::::				

1st person singular

Yes	::::::::::	I	::::::::::	::::::::::	work.
?			::::::::::	::::::::::	
No	::::::::::				

1st person plural

Yes	::::::::::	We	::::::::::	::::::::::	work.
?			::::::::::	::::::::::	
No	::::::::::				

Complete these short statements.

Yes, you do.   Yes, I _____ .   Yes, we _____ .
No, you _____ .   No, I _____ .   No, we _____ .

9.3 Make a stack of cards of verbs in the simple present **(read, reads, write, writes).** Use colored paper to match the slots. Help students to discover that verbs on orange paper won't work in the red slots meant for auxiliary verbs:

Reads he?

He reads not.

Work they?

Form small groups. Have each group pick some orange cards and form questions and answers.

9.4 On the board, draw a continuum for adverbs of time. Initial your position on the line and invite students to go to the board and do the same:

Do you use the seat belts in a car?

To demonstrate the position of adverbs of frequency in a graphic way, assign them the color code purple and insert them into the diagram in activity 9.2:

He usually works.

Does he usually work?

Have the students look in the dictionary for synonyms like **not often, hardly ever.**

9.5 Teach students to associate adverbs of frequency with all verbs in the present tense. All of you make a long list of verbs on the board. Have each person draw a continuum similar to the one in activity 9.4. Under each adverb have them show how often they engage in the activities listed on the board.

Example: he/she

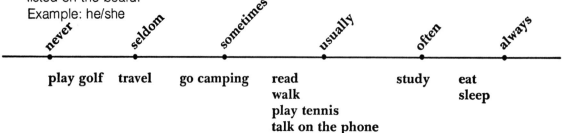

never	seldom	sometimes	usually	often	always
play golf	travel	go camping	read	study	eat
			walk		sleep
			play tennis		
			talk on the phone		

Draw the same continuum again. This time, list the verbs in the appropriate place for a good friend or some member of your family.

Example:

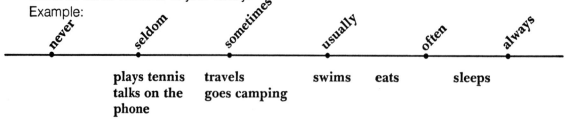

never	seldom	sometimes	usually	often	always
	plays tennis	travels	swims	eats	sleeps
	talks on the	goes camping			
	phone				

Choose partners and talk about the activities. Encourage them to make some contrasts.

I never study.

My sister always studies.

You sometimes study.

9.6 To teach the alveolar fricative endings /s/, /z/, /iz/, which mark the third person singular of verbs in the simple present, have all the students write on the board a list of the things their partner does.

    __Mike__ skis.

_____ plays ball.

_____ jogs.

_____ watches television.

_____ eats.

_____ sleeps.

On one side of the board, draw three columns for voiceless /s/, voiced /z/, and /iz/, and ask the students to read the verbs aloud and write them in the appropriate columns. Refer to Reproduction Page 5 (Activity 3.4) and help students discover:

- That verbs ending in palatal consonants **(s, z, ch, dg [j], sh)** end with **-es** (pronounced /iz/) when the subject is **he, she, it;**
- That verbs ending in other voiceless consonants add voiceless **s;**
- That verbs ending in other voiced consonants also add **s,** but are pronounced voiced /z/.

9.7 Plan a people hunt. Give everyone a copy of Reproduction Page 20, **"Find Someone Who ...."** Give students time to write the questions that they must ask in order to get the information they need.

REPRODUCTION PAGE 20

CHAPTER 2, ACTIVITY 9.7

FIND SOMEONE WHO...

Walk around and ask people questions in order to find someone who....

1. plays tennis.	Do you play tennis? John	plays tennis.
2. talks a lot.	Do you	a lot?
3. frequently goes camping.		?
4. laughs a lot.		?
5. seldom tells jokes.	Do you often	?
6. dances.		?
7. usually wears blue jeans.		?
8. always locks the door at night.		?
9. seldom watches T.V.		?
10. often eats in restaurants.		?

9.8 Use interview questions to help students understand that the simple present tense without an adverb of time suggests "normally, generally, regularly."

Do you smoke?
Do you work?

Form small groups for interviewing each other. Make the process of forming groups fun by playing the game Ducks and Cows (see Chapter 1). Whisper to students the name of the animal whose sound they are to imitate. Tell five or six people to be ducks, five or six to be cows, and whatever additional animals you need for your size class. (Be mindful of any cultural taboos regarding some animals, such as dogs.) Have students close their eyes, make their animal's sound, and walk around to find others with the same sound in order to form groups.

Each group selects a leader to interview the others in the group. Hand out copies of Reproduction Page 21, **"What Do You Do?"**

---

173   REPRODUCTION PAGE 21

                                             CHAPTER 2, ACTIVITY 9.8

WHAT DO YOU DO?

1. Do you watch television very much? What is one of your favorite programs?
2. Do you read a lot? What do you read?
3. Do you think that grades help you to learn?
4. What are you going to do during the next vacation?
5. Do you learn more in school or outside of school?
6. Do your parents buy records? What kind of records do they buy? Do you buy records?
7. How do you get money to spend?
8. Do you know what you want to do some day?
9. Do you celebrate Thanksgiving or Christmas? How do you celebrate them?
10. Do you work? Where do you work?
11. Do you smoke? Do you want to quit smoking?
12. Do you often go to museums? What kind of museums do you go to?
13. Where do you listen to music?
14. Do you go to concerts? With whom?
15. Do you know how to ski? Do you want to learn?
16. Do you know how to play the guitar? Do you want to learn?
17. Do you know the director of the school?
18. Do you or does someone in your family know a famous person?
19. Who knows you very well?
20. Do you give many parties?
21. Do you go to many parties? Do you dance?
22. Do you study alone or with friends?
23. Do you write letters? To whom do you write?

9.9 Based on Reproduction Page 21, have students write compositions on the topic, "What Do I Do?"

9.10 Invite a visitor to the class (another student or teacher, a parent, or someone in the community). Have each student plan five questions to ask the visitor, and have them write their questions and their own answers beforehand. Remind students not to ask the visitor questions that they themselves cannot or would not answer (see Chapter 1, Interviews).

9.11 Test students' mastery of the simple present tense.

Oral and Written Test Idea

Write ten questions to interview a partner in the class about what he or she does and when and how often he or she does it. After the interview write a paragraph about the other person.

Topic 10 "What do you like?"

The verb like with a complement (noun, pronoun, or infinitive)

10.1 Teach the verb **like** with foods such as popcorn, pizza, ice cream, hamburgers, candy, potato chips, and ask if they like each food.

Teacher	Student
Do you like ice cream?	**Yes, I like it.**
Do you like pizza?	**Yes, I like it.**
Do you like yogurt?	**No, I don't like it.**
Do you like hamburgers?	**Yes, I like them.**
Do you like peanuts?	**Yes, I like them.**

Guide students to provide answers using the complete grammar structure. Later they can learn to use the short answers, **Yes, I do. No, I don't.**

10.2 From magazines or newspapers, have students cut out pictures of foods they like. Help them make a poster and learn the names of the foods.

Each of you find a partner. With your own partner, provide some statements and questions as a model to initiate a conversation:

> **I like apples and oranges.**
> **I prefer apples.**
> **Do you like ice cream?**
> **Do you like candy?**
> **Which do you prefer?**

Let partners talk as freely as they like. Encourage them to find appropriate pictures and point to them.

Take every opportunity to encourage students to move around the classroom for total physical response to the language learning. Teach them to point to things, get up and show you, gesture, and demonstrate what they mean with actions. Encourage students to sit next to different people and be in different groups so that they have more opportunities to learn from each other as well as from you.

10.3 In groups of two or three, have students look through magazines and books for pictures of activities and have them ask each other:

> **What is he/she doing?**
> **Do you like to ___ski___?**

Encourage them to ask you what the word is for what a person is doing.

10.4 Everyone (teacher included) draw a picture of what you like to do. Tape the pictures to the wall and talk about each of them, using functional grammar questions (see Chapter 1, Audio Visual Method):

> **Who is this?**
>
> **What is he/she doing?**
>
> **Does he/she like to ___skate___ ?**
>
> **Do you like to ___run___ ?**

10.5 In a conversation circle, ask:

> **What do you like to do and how do you feel when you are doing it?**

Recall students' answers:

> ___Karen___ **, you like to___ski___ . You feel___happy___ when you are**
>
> ___skiing___ **.**

10.6 Give the students a worksheet made from Reproduction Page 22, **"A People Hunt."** You might like to plan one of your own in the class, letting students make suggestions as to what to include

---

REPRODUCTION PAGE 22

CHAPTER 2, ACTIVITY 10.6

A PEOPLE HUNT

Walk around asking questions like the following in order to find someone who likes a particular thing:

Do you like ice cream?

Do you like to swim?

Complete each sentence with the name of a different person.

1. _ _   likes ice cream.

2.   likes chocolates.

3.   likes cheese.

4.   likes strawberries.

5.   likes to cook.

6.   . likes to go fishing.

7.   likes to paint.

8.   likes to swim.

9.   _ likes to go camping.

10.   likes school.

10.7 Give students copies of Reproduction Page 23, **"Ten Things I Like to Do,"** and have them list the ten things. Then mark M or F in the next column if their parents like to do the same thing.

REPRODUCTION PAGE 23

CHAPTER 2, ACTIVITY 10.7

TEN THINGS I LIKE TO DO

| | My parents like to do it. | | Initial Cost | $$$ Each Time |
	Mother	Father		
1.				
2.				
3.				
4.				
5.				
6.				
7.				
8.				
9.				
10.				

Then ask if it costs money to do it, $$$ if it costs money each time, or $ if it is an initial expense (like buying equipment).

When the lists are completed, ask for a volunteer to write his or her list on the board. Then have the whole group interview that person, using questions suggested by the activities, parents' interests, cost, how often and how recently done.

Afterwards, choose partners and interview each other.

10.8 To help students prepare to talk about themselves give them copies of Reproduction Page 24, **"Who Are You?"** Complete the worksheet all together. Read each item aloud and each of you put a check mark next to the statement that applies to you.

10.9 Get into groups of three or four and each of you speak to the others in the group, for one or two minutes, on what kind of person you are.

10.10 Have students write a composition on the topic of who they are, guided by the worksheet from Reproduction Page 24.

REPRODUCTION PAGE 24

CHAPTER 2, ACTIVITY 10.8

WHO ARE YOU?

Put a check mark next to any statement that you feel describes you.

1.	am quiet.
2.	like to be alone.
3.	talk a lot.
4.	am a good listener.
5.	like to go camping.

6.	like sports.
7.	like to learn new things.
8.	like to sing.
9.	like to dance.
10.	like to draw or paint.
11.	like to make things.
12.	read a lot.
13.	never read unless I have to.
14.	enjoy arguing.
15.	do anything to avoid an argument.
16.	like to laugh.
17.	like advice from my friends.
18.	like advice from my teachers.
19.	like to give advice.
20.	like to talk things out.
21.	am easy to get along with.
22.	fight when I don't like something.
23.	think people are fun to be with.
24.	am friendly.
25.	usually like what I am doing.
26.	know how to make things interesting for myself.
27.	don't feel happy until my work is done.
28.	tell jokes.
29.	am bored easily.
30.	can be trusted.
31.	like to correct others.
32.	help others with their work.
33.	like to tell others what to do.

10.11 Test students' use of the verb **like** in statements and questions.

Oral Test Idea

Give a small-group test. Everyone has to participate for the group to get a passing grade. Make up a questionnaire to take a poll of teachers in the school and of students in the school. Some sample questions:

> **Do you like school?**
>
> **Do you prefer to read or talk in class?**
>
> **Which do you like best: cars, motorcycles, or bicycles?**
>
> **Do you prefer oral or written exams?**
>
> **At parties, do you like to dance, sing, talk, or listen to music?**

Plan an oral report to class on your findings.

Written Test Idea

> **What do you or your friends like to do at these places?**

> at home   at the swimming pool
> at parties   at church
> down town   outside
> at the lake

Write ten sentences like these:

> **I like ___to eat at parties___ .**
>
> **My friend _____ .**
>
> **My family _____ .**
>
> **_____ and I _____ .**

Topic 11 "Tell me what to do!"

Giving directions, polite commands, let's, the imperative

11.1 Using techniques of the Silent Way (see Chapter 1), help students learn to give directions or commands, using Cuisenaire rods or other objects. Work with the verbs **put, take, give.**

Sit in groups of three and give each group a handful of colored rods. Demonstrate with your own group what you want the students to do:

> **Paul, take two brown rods.**
>
> **Put them on the table.**
>
> **Take two orange rods.**
>
> **Put them on top of the brown ones.**
>
> **Chris, take two black rods.**
>
> **Give the black rods to Paul.**
>
> **Tell Paul what to do.**

If students do not understand your commands, guide their hands to carry out your instructions.

Let each student, in turn, give another student directions for building with the rods. Give them new vocabulary when they ask for it.

11.2 Use an audiovisual dialog to help students learn to give directions for going some place. Make a transparency from Reproduction Page 1. Use an overhead projector to show the pictures and explain the following dialog, using audiovisual techniques described in Chapter 1. Have two people record the dialog—native speakers of English if possible, otherwise two advanced students.

> **1.** *Tourist (a man):*   **Excuse me, please. Where is the post office?**
>
> **2.** *Clerk (a woman):* **Go out the door and turn right.**
>
> **3.** *Clerk:*   **Go straight ahead for two blocks.**
>
> **4.** *Clerk:*   **Turn left at the traffic light.**
>
> **5.** *Clerk:*   **When you get to the drugstore, cross the street.**
>
> **6.** *Clerk:*   **The post office is across from the drugstore.**
>
> **7.** *Tourist:*   **Thank you very much. Good-bye.**

Project the pictures on a screen or on the classroom wall. Set the tape recorder next to the screen and play the entire dialog. Rewind and play it again, following this procedure:

1. Looking at the lesson plan, ask the first question.
2. Play the line of tape-recorded dialog again so the students can find the words that answer the question.
3. Signal a student to answer. Do *not* talk between the time the tape is played and the student answers.
4. Repeat the question and have several students answer it.
5. Continue the same procedure for lines 2 through 7.

1. Play the tape:

Excuse me, please. Where is the post office?

Teacher		Student
What is this? (Point to the post office.)	tape	**(It's) a post office.**
Does the tourist know where the post office is?	tape	**No, he doesn't.**
Does the clerk know where the post office is?	tape	**Yes, he does.**
Ask the clerk where the post office is.	tape	**Excuse me, please. Where is the post office?**

2. Play the tape:

Go out that door and turn right.

Teacher		Student
What is this? (Point to the door.)	tape	**(It's) a door.**
Is he going out the door or coming in the door? (Point to the drawing of the man in the doorway.)	tape	**He's going out the door.**
Is he going to turn right or left?	tape	**He's going to turn right.**
Tell him to turn right.	tape	**Turn right.**
Tell him to go out the door and turn right.	tape	**Go out the door and turn right.**

3. Play the tape:

Go straight ahead for two blocks.

Teacher		Student
What is this? (Point to the block between streets.)	tape	**(It's) a block.**
How many blocks is this? (Point to the two blocks.)	tape	**Two blocks.**
Is he going straight ahead, to the right, or to the left?	tape	**Straight ahead.**
What direction is he going in?	tape	**He's going straight ahead.**
Tell him to go straight ahead for two blocks.	tape	**Go straight ahead for two blocks.**

4. Play the tape:

Turn left at the traffic light.

Teacher		Student
What is this? (Point to the traffic light.)	tape	**(It's) a traffic light.**

What should he do at the traffic light?	tape	**Turn left.**
Should he turn left?	tape	**Yes, he should turn left.**
Tell him what to do at the traffic light.	tape	**Turn left at the traffic light.**

5. Play the tape:

When you get to the drugstore, cross the street.

Teacher		Student
What is this? (Point to the drugstore.)	tape	**It's a drugstore.**
And what is this? (Point to the street.)	tape	**It's a street.**
What is he going to do?	tape	**He's going to cross the street.**
When is he going to cross the street?	tape	**When he gets to the drugstore.**
Give him instructions.	tape	**When you get to the drugstore, cross the street.**

6. Play the tape:

The post office is across from the drugstore.

Teacher		Student
What is across the street from the post office?	tape	**The drugstore.**
Where is the post office?	tape	**The post office is across from the drugstore.**

7. Play the tape:

Thank you very much. Good-bye.

Teacher		Student
Thank the clerk.	tape	**Thank you very much.**
What do you say when you leave?	tape	**Good-bye.**
Thank the clerk and leave.	tape	**Thank you very much. Good-bye.**

11.3 Give directions for going from the school to your house. Choose a partner and give directions while your partner draws a map on the board. Have students choose a partner and have them give directions while the partner draws a map.

11.4 Have students help you think of commands they hear during the day and have them write two lists on the board (with identifying drawings if necessary):

What are some commands at school?

What are some commands at home?

Don't overlook the happy commands, like:

Come and eat.

Choose partners. Go back over the lists and repeat each command, waiting while the partners say it to each other. Ask:

How do you feel?

And let different students answer.

11.5 Test students' mastery of the future with **going to** and the imperative.

Reading and Writing Test Idea

1. Read the following instructions for going someplace in the school.
2. Write about what you are going to do.
3. Follow the instructions, find the place, and get your "treat."

Write out several sets of instructions for students to get to various places in the school, such as the history classroom, counselor's office, library, secretary's office, principal's office, chemistry laboratory. Arrange in advance for someone at each location to give students a treat when they arrive.

Sample instructions:

Go out the classroom door. Turn right. Go straight ahead along the hall until you get to the next hallway. Turn left. Pass the gymnasium and go up the stairs. Go into the office on the left. Ask the secretary if she has something for you. Please come back quickly!
"What are you going to do?"
"I'm going to go out the classroom door. I'm going to turn . . ."

Oral Test Idea

Think of ten commands or invitations that you like or would like to hear. Tell them to a partner and see if he or she likes them too.

Topic 12   "What did you do?"

Simple past tense and expressions of time

12.1 Teach the past with one of Carolyn Graham's *Jazz Chants.** Use a tape recording with audiovisual techniques to help students with the difficult pronunciation problems presented by words with two or three consonants clustered at the end. Make a transparency of illustrations on Reproduction Page 25, **"A Bad Day."**

> **1. I overslept and missed my train,**
>
> **2. Slipped on the sidewalk in the pouring rain.**
>
> **3. Broke my glasses, lost my keys,**

---

*A well-recorded tape cassette is available with the book. The poem is reprinted from *Jazz Chants: Rhythms of American English for Students of English as a Second Language* by Carolyn Graham. Copyright 1978 by Oxford University Press, Inc. Reprinted by permission.

REPRODUCTION PAGE 25

CHAPTER 2, ACTIVITY 12.1

A BAD DAY

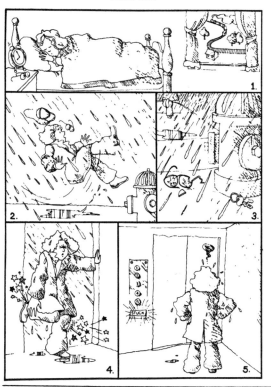

4. Sprained my ankle, skinned my knees.
5. Got stuck in the elevator; it wouldn't go.
6. Kicked it twice and stubbed my toe.
7. Bought a pen; it wouldn't write.
8. Took it back and had a fight.
9. Went home angry, locked the door.
10. Crawled into bed, couldn't take any more.

REPRODUCTION PAGE 25 (continued)

CHAPTER 2, ACTIVITY 12.1.

A BAD DAY (2)

Plan questions that will help students understand both the grammar and the vocabulary of each line of the poem. Review the techniques of audiovisual methodology in Chapter 1.

Write detailed lesson plans.

1. Play the tape:

I overslept and missed my train,

Teacher		Student
What is this? (Point to the train.)	tape	**It's a train.**
What is she doing? (Point to the girl sleeping.)	tape	**She is sleeping.**
What did she do?	tape	**She overslept.**
What happened?	tape	**She missed the train.**
Carolyn, what did you do?	tape	**I overslept and missed the train.**

2. Play the tape:

Slipped on the sidewalk in the pouring rain.

Teacher		Student
What's this? (Point to the sidewalk.)	tape	**It's a sidewalk.**
What's this? (Point to the rain.)	tape	**It's the rain.**
Is it a light rain shower? (Point to the pouring rain.)	tape	**It's a pouring rain.**
What did she do? (Point to the girl.)	tape	**She slipped.**
Where did she slip?	tape	**She slipped on the sidewalk.**
Carolyn, what did you do?	tape	**I slipped on the sidewalk in the pouring rain.**

3. Play the tape:

Broke my glasses, lost my keys,

Teacher		Student
What are these? (Point to the keys.)	tape	**They're keys.**
Whose keys are they?		**They're her keys.**
What are these? (Point to the glasses.)	tape	**They're glasses.**
Whose glasses are they?		**They're her glasses.**
Carolyn, what did you do?	tape	**I broke my glasses, lost my keys.**

Continue through the rest of the poem, making up lesson plans like these.

12.2 Teach students when to use the past **-ed** and when to use the past auxiliary **did**. On a wall chart draw a diagram similar to those you have used before, and color code it to compare with the others (see Activities 4.1, 9.2).

	(red)	*(blue)*	*(red)*	*(yellow)*	*(orange)*
Yes		**He**			worked.
	Did	he			work?
?	**Didn't**	he			work?
No		**He**		did	n't	work.

Erase the verb **work** and let the students write other verbs in that space.

Erase **he** and write in the other personal pronouns, including **it,** so students can see that the verb remains the same with all persons.

12.3 Contrast the present with the past, asking questions like these:

Where do you live now? Did you live there when you were a child?

Did you play ball when you were a child? Do you play ball now?

Did you have a pet when you were a child? Do you have one now?

Give the students copies of Reproduction Page 26, **"Childhood,"** help them make up questions similar to those above, and continue with small-group interviews.

REPRODUCTION PAGE 26

CHAPTER 2, ACTIVITY 12.3

CHILDHOOD

1. When you were a child, where did you live?
2. Did you live in the country or in the city?
3. Did you sleep upstairs or downstairs?
4. Did you share your bedroom with anyone?
5. Did you play ball?
6. Did you play with dolls?
7. What games did you play?
8. Did you like school?
9. Did you study a lot?
10. Did lots of people visit your family?
11. Did you learn a lot at school?
12. Did you play a musical instrument?
13. Did you practice a lot?
14. Did you visit your grandparents?
16. Where did they live?
17. Did you watch television?
18. Did you earn money? How?
19. What did you want to be when you grew up?
20. How many people lived in your house?
21. What was your best friend's name?

12.4 Interview one of the students about his or her childhood. Begin the interview yourself, but encourage the other students to ask questions also. Then choose partners and interview each other. Afterwards, tell the large group something about your partner.

Remind the students of the two basic rules for interviews (see Chapter 1):

1. The person interviewed can always decline to answer, saying simply, **"I pass."**

2. The person interviewed can ask the interviewer the same questions and he or she *must* answer.

12.5 Complete these sentences and share one with the group:

When I was a child, I believed _____ .

I wanted _____ .

I liked _____ .

I had to _____ .

I hated _____ .

I believed _____ .

12.6 Write the following questions on the board, using irregular verbs. Have students interview you, then each other, in groups of five:

When you were a child, what were your favorite holidays?

Did you go somewhere to celebrate?

Did you have a holiday dinner?

Where did you eat?

Did adults and children eat together?

Were many people there?

What did the children do?

Did you like those reunions?

Which holiday did you like best?

12.7 In a conversation circle, ask:

When you were a child, what were you afraid of?

As a child, what did you do for fun that you don't do now?

What did you want to be that you don't want to be now?

12.8 Have students help you make a long list of verbs on the board. Then have them write the past tense beside each verb.

Have each student write the title "Past Tense Verb Endings" on a sheet of paper; dividing the page into four columns, heading the columns, **voiceless /t/, voiced /d/, /ĭd/, irregular.** List the past tense forms of the verbs that are on the board in the appropriate categories according to their endings.
Example:

voiceless /t/	voiced /d/	/ĭd/	irregular
fished	learned	petted	swam
cooked	studied	repeated	ate
	played		went

When the students finish their lists, have them form groups of three or four to check each other's classifications and come to some agreement on what is correct and perhaps draw some conclusions as to why. Guide them to consult **"English Vowels and Consonants,"** Reproduction Page 2, activity 3.1, and notice that:

1. The sound /t/ follows voiceless consonants.
2. The sound /d/ follows voiced consonants and vowels.
3. The sound /ĭd/ follows the letters **t** and **d.**

12.9 Help students realize that the speaker has some particular time in mind when using the simple past tense. Interview the whole group. Remind them that they always have the option of passing and that at the end of the interview they can ask you questions if they would like to:

Did you visit some friends yesterday?

Did you write anything last night?

Where did you eat last night? Who ate with you?

Did you go out last night? Did you have a good time?

What movie did you see last month?

Did you smoke a cigarette this morning?

> **Did you brush your teeth this morning?**
> **What kind of toothpaste did you use?**
> **Did you learn something in this class yesterday?**
> **Did you like something yesterday?**
> **Did something new or good happen to you? Explain.**

12.10 Practice using more irregular verbs. With the class in small groups, give the leader of each group these questions for interviewing members of the group:

> **Did you go somewhere last summer?**
> **Who went? Did you like your trip?**
> **Who decided where you were going to go?**
> **What did you see?**
> **Did you have a good time?**

12.11 Find a partner and ask each other the following question:

> **How did you spend last Sunday?**

The two find another couple in order to talk about the previous week's activities. Have the group choose a leader and give the leader these two questions to ask of each one in the group:

> **What did you do last week that you liked?**
> **What did you do last week that you didn't like?**

12.12 Plan to invite a visitor to the class to be interviewed. Let the students decide who (another student, a parent, someone in the community, a teacher from another class, or another staff member). Ask students to prepare some questions in advance for the visitor.

12.13 An excellent activity for developing confidence is the Trust Walk, a nonverbal activity in which each participant walks with eyes closed, depending on a partner for guidance (see Chapter 1). Introduce the activity to the students in this way:

> **How do we communicate? We communicate not only by talking but also by touching, smelling, tasting, and hearing. We're going to have an experience in communicating without talking or seeing, without using our voice or our eyes.**

Ask each student to find a partner. The two of them are going to walk around, one leading and the other being led, with his or her eyes closed. They will communicate with one another without talking and one without seeing either.

The one who is leading should try to make the activity as interesting and as much fun as possible. The leader could have his or her partner touch objects that might be a surprise, like something cold or wet; could have the partner smell things; could make slow and fast movements (being careful to guide the partner so as not to have an accident).

Set the limits as broad as possible, such as inside the school building or within the school grounds. After ten minutes ask the students to exchange roles so that each one will experience both leading and being led. Ask them to return to the group in twenty minutes. Back in the large group, discuss the following questions with partners and then share some observations with the whole group.

> **Did something surprise you?**
> **Which did you like better: leading or being led?**

Did anything frighten you?

Did you learn anything about yourself or your partner?

Is there anything that you didn't understand?

12.14 Plan a field trip to some place that class members are interested in visiting. It could be an unfamiliar area of the school, such as the industrial arts shop, the home economics room, the radio station; or it could be outside the school: a restaurant, someone's house, an interesting local store, a museum. Help the students plan some interview questions and think of things to look for at their destination. They could go alone or in small groups. See Real-Life Experiences, Chapter 1, and Understanding Other Cultures, Chapter 3. After their excursion, have students report their observations and feelings, using the worksheets prepared from Reproduction Page 27, **"How Was Your Field Trip?"**

REPRODUCTION PAGE 27

CHAPTER 2, ACTIVITY 12.14

HOW WAS YOUR FIELD TRIP?

1. How did you decide with whom to go? Did you decide to go alone, be with friends, go with people you didn't know at all? Explain.

2. Write a summary of what you did. How did you go? With whom? What did you do there?

3. Thinking about your experience, complete these sentences.

When	I felt
When	I felt
When	I felt
When	I felt
When	I felt

4. What did you do for the first time? How did you feel?

5. What did you want to do differently: talk to more people, be there longer, be more involved? Why didn't you do it?

6. Make a list of seven words that you associate with the place where you went.

7. Pick one or two of the following sentences to finish.

I learned that

I was surprised that

I remembered that

I relearned that

I realized that

I observed that

12.15 Test students' use of the past tense.

Written Test Idea

Having them refer to the questions on Reproduction Page 26 (see Activity 12.3 above), ask students to write a composition about their childhood.

Oral Test Ideas

1. Have students present a brief talk based on their written composition about their childhood. Suggest that the students use visual aids to add interest.

2. Ask students to describe a game they played when they were children and, if possible, to teach it to the class.

Topic 13 "What do you have?" "Who gave it to you?"

Verbs have and give; determiners; objects and object pronouns

13.1 Contrast the indefinite object pronoun **one** and the definite pronoun **it** and teach the verb **have,** using Cuisenaire rods or colored pencils (see Chapter 1). Sit in a circle with the students and put some rods, one of each color, in the center. Take a rod yourself and tell a student:

Take a rod.

Indicate that she should give the same instruction to someone else and continue around the circle until all the rods are gone. Say:

I have a rod. __Bob__ doesn't have one. __Cindy__ has one.

Who else has one?

Each student responds in one of two ways:

I have one. (or) **I don't have one.**

__Cindy__ has one. (or) **__Bob__ doesn't have one.**

Then ask:

Who has the red rod?

Make sure that the answer is definite:

I have it. (or) **__Ed__ has it.**

Signal the students to continue asking each other about all the colors.

13.2 Still using the colored rods or a number of other objects, teach the determiners **many, a lot of (lots of),** and **a few:**

I have six rods. __Quasim__, how many rods do you have? Do you have lots of rods?

__Salim__ doesn't have many rods. He has only a few.

__Anna__ has a lot of rods. She has a few blue ones and lots of red ones. How many greens ones does she have?

Encourage the students to express similar comments and questions about what they have. Seated around a large table, let the whole class work together, taking turns talking. Or divide the class into smaller groups at tables. Go from group to group to check on their understanding and use of these determiners.

13.3 Contrast **How many?** and **How much?** Put a number of items on a table and have the students ask appropriate questions:

How much paper is there? How many sheets of paper are there?

How much money is there? How many coins are there?

How much water is there? How many cups of water are there?

By this time students should have discovered that they use:

How many? when they are referring to things that can be counted one, two, three, four.

How much? when they are referring to something that cannot be counted without breaking it up into countable pieces.

How *much money?*   How *many dollars?*

How *much bread?*   How *many loaves of bread?*

To learn to answer the questions, use a continuum.

How *much time* do you spend watching television?

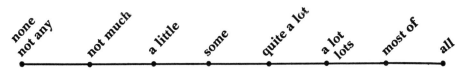

How *many books* do you have?

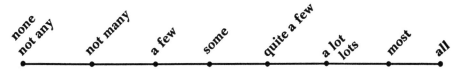

Get into small groups and have the students make up **How much?** and **How many?** questions for using with a continuum. When each group has one, let a group member write it on the board for everyone to initial his or her answer.

13.4 Have each student choose a partner to interview about things they have. Have students sit down with their partners and listen while you interview your partner, as a model, with questions like these:

Do you have a pet? What is it?

Do you have a favorite record?

How many brothers and sisters do you have?

Do you have a favorite class?

Do you have a favorite teacher?

Do you have a favorite place where you like to be? What is it?

Partners interview each other and then return to the large group to tell something about each other.

13.5 To teach indirect object pronouns and their position in the sentence, plan a lesson like the Example of Oral Grammar Manipulation in Chapter 1.

Teacher: **Mike has my pencil. Who gave it to him?**

Student: **You gave it to him.**

Teacher: **Did he give it to me?**

Student: **No, you gave it to him.**

Teacher: **Mike, did I give my pencil to you?**

Student: **Yes, you gave it to me.**

> *Teacher:*   **Ask Mike who gave the pencil to him.**
> *Student:*   **Mike, who gave the pencil to you?**
> *Student:*   **Ginny gave it to me.**

13.6 Ask students to think of things they want or don't want as they practice the use of the direct object pronouns **it** and **them.** Give the students copies of Reproduction Page 28, **"Do You Want It?"**

REPRODUCTION PAGE 28

CHAPTER 2, ACTIVITY 13.6

DO YOU WANT IT?

Fill in appropriate questions and your answers.

1. I would like to give you a guitar. Do you want it?
   No, thank you, I don't want it.

2. I would like to give you some flowers. Do you want them?
   Yes, give them to me please.

3. I would like to give you a water bed. _____ ?
   _____ .

4. I would like to give you some cookies. _____ ?
   _____ .

5. I would like to give you a sports car. _____ ?
   _____ .

6. I would like to give you a Spanish dictionary. _____ ?
   _____ .

7. I would like to give you an English dictionary. _____ ?
   _____ .

8. I would like to give you some new skis. _____ ?
   _____ .

9. I would like to give you a motorcycle. _____ ?
   _____ .

10. I would like to give you a ten-speed bike. _____ ?
    _____ .

11. I would like to give you some vitamins. _____
    _____ .

12. I would like to give you a hamburger. _____ ?
    _____ .

13.7 After completing the previous activity, have students get into groups with each one thinking of something they would like to give to another. Use questions and answers similar to those on Reproduction Page 8, **"Do You Want It?"**

13.8 In a conversation circle, ask:

> **What do you have that you like? Who gave it to you?**

Afterwards, recall:

> ___Mercedes___ , you have a ___book___ . Your friend gave it to you.

13.9 List things that you have to do. Example:

> **eat**
>
> **sleep**

study

go to school

work

List your activities in appropriate places on the following continuum.

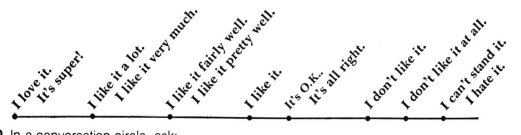

13.10 In a conversation circle, ask:

What do you have to do that you don't like, and how does it make you feel?

13.11 Write your own simple composition and give students copies to read and use as a model for similar compositions. Model:

I have several things that are important to me. I have a husband and children to love. I have a mind to think with. I have a pleasant place to live. I'm very happy.

When students come to class the next day, have them read their papers to each other and use them as a stimulus for conversation (see Chapter 1, Reading).

13.12 Prepare reading material from small-group conversations. Record students talking with each other, transcribe the conversations, and make copies to read aloud the following day. Have the participants read their parts as in a play. To do this, refer to the techniques of Counseling-Learning in Chapter 1. Seat a small group, no more than six, in a circle with a tape recorder and microphone in the middle. Don't place yourself in the circle, but stand just outside to give any necessary assistance. The following are two different ways to conduct and record a conversation:

　　　1. With the microphone in the center of the group, let the students talk—expressing themselves any way they can in order to be understood—and record it verbatim. Afterwards, the teacher transcribes the conversation, translating it into standard English.

　　　2. The student who wants to talk says what he or she wants to say and listens to the teacher express it in standard English. Then the student turns on the hand-held microphone, repeats the sentence, and turns off the microphone. Another student repeats the procedure. Afterwards, students listen to the tape and transcribe their own conversation.

13.13 Test students' use of **have** and **give** with complements.

Written Test Idea

List five people to whom you would like to give something, and tell why. Model:

I would like to give my son a new car. I would like to give him one because someone stole his.

Oral Test Idea

Prepare a half-minute talk about what people have that is important to them. Model:

Teachers have books. My dog has his bed. Some people have dishwashers. We have the responsibility to vote.

Topic 14   "What are you like?"

Adjectives with comparison; nouns formed from adjectives and verbs

14.1 Interview a student. Model:

What color are the walls of your bedroom?

What is your favorite color?

What color is your favorite shirt or dress?

Which room in your house is your favorite?

What color are the walls of that room?

How do you feel in that room? Are you contented, excited, happy, peaceful?

If students have difficulty understanding, demonstrate the meaning by pointing to things, to pictures, or to a house plan. Use your own answers to the questions as a model.

Form small groups of two to four students and have them interview each other. Write some questions on the board to help them.

14.2 Use color to talk about customs and feelings. What colors do you associate with weddings, newborn babies, funerals? Compare colors with feelings, using nouns derived from adjectives. Lay out a selection of colored markers and let students color as you talk:

What color is happiness?

What color is sadness?

What color is excitement?

What color is boredom?

What color is anger?

What color is death?

Of course answers will vary, according to individual interpretations as well as cultural differences.

Draw a line for a continuum entitled, How Are You Today? (see activity 5.6). Have students write their names on the line, using colored markers to represent their feelings.

14.3 Help students learn how to deal with numbers:

When is your birthday?

How old are you?

How much do you weigh?

Remember that each one has the choice not to answer. You might discuss when and how it is socially acceptable or taboo to ask these questions. Of course, people are publicly requested to answer each of these questions on questionnaires such as an application for a driver's license. You might like to bring in driver's license application forms and fill them in.

Bring a tape measure and measure students' height in feet and inches and also in centimeters. Compare weight in pounds and kilograms.

Write birthdays on a classroom calendar and remember to celebrate them.

14.4 Make comparisons. Give each person a worksheet prepared from Reproduction Page 29, **"Comparisons."**

Bring the class together for a group interview, asking questions quickly around the class:

Who is taller than you?

Who is shorter than you?

Finish with:

Who is the tallest one in the class?

Who is the shortest?

Who is the oldest?

Who is the youngest?

Are men stronger than women?

REPRODUCTION PAGE 29

CHAPTER 2, ACTIVITY 14.4

COMPARISONS

Walk around the room, talking to other students and making comparisons. Write answers to the questions using as many students' names as possible.

1. Who is taller than you are?   is taller than I am.

2. Who is as tall as you?

3. Who is shorter than you

4. Who is stronger than you are?

5. Who is happier than you are today?

6. Who is more active than you are?

7. Who is studying more than you are in this class?

8. Who talks more often in English than you do?

9. Who is more daring than you are?

10. Who is more careful than you are?

11. Who is as dependable as you are?

14.5 Have students help you make a list on the board of the ways people learn, using the noun form of verbs: _____-ing. Ask:

How do you learn? By studying, by listening to the teacher. How else do you learn?

Make sure that the list includes:

> **memorizing**
> **thinking**
> **experimenting**
> **doing what the teacher says**

Then each of you select from the list ways that you find you learn the best and rank them in the order of importance for you. Tell the students that you are going to keep the papers to help you plan lessons.

14.6 Identify everyone's astrological sign. Read a simple horoscope for each sign represented in the class and all of you compare yourselves with your horoscope:

> **I'm like that.**
> **I'm not like that.**

This exercise helps people look objectively at themselves and others in an accepting, non-judgmental way.

14.7 Describe a tree in a novel way. Take the class outside to a tree. Divide the class into two groups and give the members of one group the assignment of observing the tree from varying points of view: one far away, another lying under the tree, one close to the tree, another hugging the trunk of the tree. Have each one describe the tree, using one or two words. Have the second group collect the words and combine them into a description of the tree. The results can be quite poetic; it is creative writing with the minimum amount of language. (See *Write Now: Insights into Creative Writing* in the resources section for teaching writing, Chapter 1.)

14.8 Using copies of Reproduction Page 30, **"How Do You Feel?"** have students think of adjectives that describe someone who is important in their lives. Write a model paragraph, describing someone who is or has been important in your life. Ask students to do the same; the next day have them read their compositions aloud to a partner.

14.9 Choose ten adjectives from Reproduction Page 30 in activity 14.8 and write a sentence with each one. Model:

> **I am ___proud___ when I ___think of a new idea___ .**
> **I am _____ when _____.**

Read your sentences to the students and have them each write ten similar sentences. The next day have them choose partners and share their sentences.

14.10 Test students' mastery of the use of adjectives and comparisons.

Written Test Idea

List ten adjectives describing yourself at school. Compare your feelings with those of a friend.

Oral Test Idea

Choose one of the following for a one-minute talk:
1. Compare yourself (size, age, feelings) with someone in your family or with a friend.
2. Compare two other people.

HOW DO YOU FEEL?

embarrassed	peaceful	inferior	joyful
frustrated	relaxed	weak	refreshed
nervous	guilty	strong	foolish
grateful	stimulated	free	happy
proud	pressured	envious	inadequate
scared	inspired	defeated	adventuresome
amazed	enthusiastic	tense	bored
angry	lonely	apathetic	boring
annoyed	healthy	sympathetic	cold
ashamed	energetic	confident	warm
excited	confused	timid	friendly
good	accepted	shy	cautious
furious	contented	brave	creative
sad	thrilled	courageous	capable
unhappy	responsible	daring	serious
depressed	indebted	generous	loving
humble	overwhelmed	clumsy	caring
calm	relieved	worthless	careful
patient	satisfied	stupid	dependable
impatient	superior	triumphant	confident
secure	insecure	loved	irritable

Topic 15   "Will you do what you can, should, and would like to do?"

Modal auxiliary verbs

15.1 Ask students a few questions about the future to help them understand the use of the future auxiliary **will:**

Will you eat dinner at home tonight?

Who will cook dinner?

What will you have?

Draw a diagram like the one for the verb **be** in activity 4.1 and the auxiliary **do** in activity 9.2.

	(red)	(blue)	(red)	(yellow)	(orange)
Yes		He	'll		cook.
		He	will		cook.
?	Will	he			cook?
	Won't	he			cook?
No		He	will	not.	cook?
		He	wo	n't	cook?

Prepare a stack of orange pieces of paper with different verbs written on them to substitute for the verb **cook** in the orange-colored verb slot. Prepare a pack of blue cards with various subjects that can be substituted in the blue-colored subject slot. Include the other personal pronouns **she, you, I, we, they** to show that the verbs don't change (unless you prefer to teach **I shall, we shall**).

Have students draw cards, substitute the subject and verb cards, and ask questions or make statements with tag questions:

Will you study German?

You'll study German, won't you?

Have students give short answers:

Yes, I will.

No, I won't.

Form small groups and give each group a stack of subject and verb cards to stimulate more questions about the future. Encourage them to think of new questions on their own.

15.2 Talk about the future using the auxiliary **will**. Give students copies of Reproduction Page 31, **"What Will You Be Like?"** Read the questions aloud and each of you answer "yes," "no," or "probably" to each question.

REPRODUCTION PAGE 31

CHAPTER 2, ACTIVITY 15.2

WHAT WILL YOU BE LIKE?

Answer "yes," or "no," or "probably" to each question.

1. Will you have six children or more?
2. Will you marry someone of a different religion?
3. Will you ever stop smoking?
4. Will you ever grow a beard? (*male*)
5. Will you ever date a man with a beard? (*female*)
6. Will you always read the sports in the newspaper?
7. Will you marry for money?
8. Will you graduate from college?
9. Will you earn a lot of money?
10. Will you be boss in your family?
11. Will you live here always?
12. Will you travel in space?
13. Will you travel to other countries?
14. Will you learn another language?
15. Will you ever smoke?
16. Will you have a big wedding?
17. Will you get fat?
18. Will you watch a lot of television when you are forty years old?
19. Will you invite people of a different race to your house?
20. Will you live on a street with people of a different race?
21. Will you marry more than once?
22. Will you surely move away from your home town?
23. Will you ever have a car?
24. Will you have trouble with the police?
25. Will you drive very fast?
26. Will you be a good father or mother?
27. Will you frequently get drunk?
28. Will you get very angry with your husband or wife?
29. Will you always go away for vacations?
30. Will you stay at home every evening?
31. Will you work after marriage?

15.3 Each one of you complete the following statements:

I am a person who will _____ .

I am a person who will never _____ .

I am a person who will probably _____ .

Everyone share one of the statements with the whole class.

15.4 Lead the students to speculate on what the world will be like five years from now. Write on the board:

In five years, what year will it be? _____ .

Get them to help you think of more questions. Then form groups of six or seven and have a leader interview the others in the group. Give each of the leaders a copy of the questions on Reproduction Page 32, **"Future."**

---

195   REPRODUCTION PAGE 32

CHAPTER 2, ACTIVITY 15.4

FUTURE

In five years . . .

1. What year will it be?
2. How old will you be?
3. Will you be living near here?
4. Will you be married?
5. Will you have any children?
6. Will you have the same job?
7. What kind of a job will you have?
8. What kind of a job would you like to have?
9. Will you be able to afford a car, a house?
10. Will you have a lot of money in the bank?
11. Will we have a Republican, Democratic, or third-party president?
12. Will the president be black? Will the president be a woman?
13. Will you be afraid of the end of the world, a civil war, or a nuclear war?
14. Will there be enough to eat in the world?
15. Will you be a vegetarian?
16. What will be the big news in the headlines?
17. How much will you pay for a loaf of bread?
18. Will cars run on gas?
19. Will every family have a plane? Will it be a jet?
20. Will we have robots?
21. Will we eat dehydrated food and capsules instead of fresh food?
22. How will ecology affect the way of life?
23. Will all clothing be unisex?
24. Will the earth be governed by an international institution?
25. Will we have shortages?
26. Will you have a computer in your home?

15.5 Using Reproduction Page 32, **"Future,"** have students write compositions of two or three paragraphs on what they think the world will be like in five years.

15.6 Demonstrate **will** as a modal verb describing willingness.
Let students offer treats to each other:

Will you (won't you) have a cookie?

Make a request:

Will you lend me your pencil?

Will you listen, please?

Show how **would** and **will** are used interchangeably. **Would** may make a request a little milder or more polite, but explain that the inflection affects the tone of the request more than do the words):

Would you listen, please?

Other uses of **would, can, should, must:**

> **Wouldn't you like to play a game?**
>
> **Can you make a ball with paper and masking tape?**
>
> **Can you throw it across the room?**
>
> **Can someone catch it?**
>
> **Must we make up some rules for the game?**
>
> **Would you like for us to learn while we play?**
>
> **Should the person throwing the ball ask a question before he or she throws the ball?**
>
> **Should he or she call the name of the person who should catch the ball?**
>
> **Would we like the ball to be caught easily each time?**
>
> **Must we throw the ball carefully so that no one will miss?**
>
> **Must the person catching the ball answer a question?**

Naturally it would be fun to play the game now.

15.7 Ask "yes" or "no" questions for everyone to answer. Mark everyone's place on a continuum, drawn on the board. **Must** represents the highest degree of certainty felt by the speaker, while **might** represents the greatest uncertainty. The shades of difference in meaning are subtle and the order on the continuum is not set by any inflexible rule. Intonation is still the decisive factor.

Will you finish an important job today?

Uncertain   *Certain*

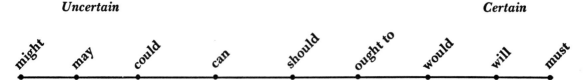

You and the students take turns making up questions for everyone to answer. Have everyone put his or her initials on the line.

15.8 Help students discover how modal verbs are used in affirmative and negative statements and questions. Give them worksheets made from Reproduction Page 33, **"Modal Verbs,"** and let them work in pairs or small groups to fill in the blank spaces.

In the small groups, have students use modal verbs to make up questions to ask each other.

15.9 Each one of you draw a large circle on a piece of paper and divide it in quarters. In each quarter, draw a sketch or a symbol representing:

Something that you can do well,

Something that you should do,

Something that you would like to do,

Something that you will do.

REPRODUCTION PAGE 33

CHAPTER 2, ACTIVITY 15.8

MODAL VERBS

Fill in the blank spaces.

Willingness	(red)	(blue)	(red)	(yellow)	(orange)
Yes		He	'll		cook
		He	will		cook
?	Will	he			cook?
	Won't	he			cook?
No		He	will	not	cook.
		He	wo	n't	cook.

Less sure willingness

	(red)	(blue)	(red)	(yellow)	(orange)
Yes		He	'd		come.
?					
	Wouldn't	he			go?
No					

Escapable obligation or duty

	(red)	(blue)	(red)	(yellow)	(orange)
Yes					
		He	should		go.
?					
No					

Inescapable obligation (has to) *Mustn't is often replaced by doesn't have to.*

	(red)	(blue)	(red)	(yellow)	(orange)
Yes					
		He	must		work.
?	✱				
No			✱		

Ability or permission

	(red)	(blue)	(red)	(yellow)	(orange)
Yes					
		He	can		swim.
?					
No					

Add a tag question to each *Yes* or *No* statement above and answer it with a short sentence. Example:

He'll cook, won't he?
Yes, he will. / No, he won't.

He won't cook, will he?
Yes, he will. / No, he won't.

Have the students draw similar sketches and share them with a partner; then change partners and share them with another.

15.10 Guide students to think about how they feel when they are doing something they want to do that is also something they need to do and can do well. Give them copies of Reproduction Page 34, **"What Can You Do Well?"** Let them have plenty of time to think of their answers. Then form small groups and discuss the answers. (You might like to use the Ducks and Cows game to form the groups. See Chapter 1.)

Finally bring the whole group together to share their answers to the last question on Reproduction Page 34.

REPRODUCTION PAGE 34

CHAPTER 2, ACTIVITY 15.10

WHAT CAN YOU DO WELL?

Answer these questions, then discuss the questions in groups of three or four.

1. What can you do well? (*Name several things.*)

2. What should you do today? (*Name several things.*)

3. What must you do today?

4. What would you like to do today?

5. How do you feel when you should do something, but you can't do it well?

6. How do you feel when you should do something but you would like to do something else?

7. Is there something that you should do, that you would like to do, and that you can do well? How do you feel when you are doing that?

15.11 Test students' mastery of modal verb auxiliaries **will, can, should, must.**

Written Test Idea

Write a short composition about something that you will do, something that you can do, should do, and would like to do.

Oral Test Idea

Make a collage—combining magazine illustrations and sketches—of how you imagine the world will be in the year 2000. Show your collage and talk about it.

Topic 16 "What have you done and when did you do it?"

Present perfect tense contrasted with simple past

16.1 Contrast the indefinite time of the present perfect tense (any time up to this moment) and the definite limit in time suggested by the simple past:

__Kazuko__, open the door, please.

Has __Kazuko__ opened the door?

When did __Kazuko__ open the door?

__Heidi__, erase the board, please.

Has __Heidi__ erased the board?

When did __Heidi__ erase the board?

Continue with other actions.

16.2 To compare statements and questions using **have,** draw a color-coded diagram similar to those you have used before:

	(red)	(blue)	(red)	(yellow)	(orange)	(green)
Yes		He He	''s has		read read	the newspaper. the newspaper.
?	Has	he			read	the newspaper?
	Hasn't	he			read	the newspaper?
No		He He	has has	not n't	read read	the newspaper. the newspaper.

Change the subject to **we** and have the students write new sentences. Have the students think of and list on the board other verbs to substitute for the principal verb in the orange slot.

In small groups, have students make up questions to ask each other. Check to see that they are using tag questions and short answers when appropriate.

16.3 Interview the students at random:

Have you traveled by train? By bus? By plane?

Have you climbed a mountain?

Have you killed a bear?

Have you played soccer?

Have you played tennis this year?

Have you skied?

Have you roller-skated?

Have you visited someone in the hospital or in a nursing home?

Have you acted in a play?

Have you cooked dinner for your family?

16.4 Provide model interview questions to practice the unusual English usage of **How long have you . . . ?**

How long have you lived here?

How long have you known me?

How long have you known your favorite teacher?

How long have you been studying English?

How long have you been going to school here? Playing the guitar? Jogging?

Have students find partners and ask each other:

Who is a good friend?

How long have you known each other?

What have you done together?

16.5 Have students take a position on a values continuum (see Chapter 1).

I have learned everything in _____ **everything outside school.** **of school.**

I have learned

Draw a line on the board and all of you initial your positions on the line.

16.6 Give students copies of Reproduction Page 35, **"Principal Parts of Irregular Verbs."** Ask students to help you make up questions, using the first group of verbs. Make up questions contrasting the present perfect (indefinite time, **have**) and the simple past (definite time, **did.**) For example:

Have you ever cut yourself?

Where did you cut yourself?

Have you ever hurt your head?

How did you hurt it?

Do you know someone who has quit school?

Why did he or she quit?

Don't try to use all the verbs; use the ones that seem natural and easy to use. Form groups of four and ask each other the questions. Then divide into groups of two and make up similar questions from group B of the verbs. Continue this activity another day with group C of the verbs.

REPRODUCTION PAGE 35

CHAPTER 2, ACTIVITY 16.6

PRINCIPAL PARTS OF IRREGULAR VERBS

Unfortunately, English is highly irregular. You'll find some patterns, but you'll have to learn them through usage.

1. The present tense, the past tense, and the past participle are the same.

cut	cut	cut
hit	hit	hit
hurt	hurt	hurt
let	let	let
put	put	put
quit	quit	quit
set	set	set
shut	shut	shut
split	split	split

REPRODUCTION PAGE 35 (continued)

CHAPTER 2, ACTIVITY 16.6

2. The past tense and past participle are the same, but different from the present tense.

build	built	built
sit	sat	sat
send	sent	sent
spend	spent	spent

feed	fed	fed
hold	held	held
read	read	read
	(pronounced / red/)	

feel	felt	felt
keep	kept	kept
leave	left	left
mean	meant	meant
meet	met	met
sleep	slept	slept
sweep	swept	swept

bring	brought	brought
catch	caught	caught
fight	fought	fought
seek	sought	sought
teach	taught	taught
think	thought	thought

bind	bound	bound
find	found	found
grind	ground	ground

get	got	got(ten)
lose	lost	lost
shoot	shot	shot

hear	heard	heard
lay	laid	laid
pay	paid	paid
make	made	made
say	said	said
sell	sold	sold
stand	stood	stood

hang	hung	hung
stick	stuck	stuck
sting	stung	stung
strike	struck	struck
swing	swung	swung
win	won	won

3. The present tense, the past tense, and the past participle are all different.

break	broke	broken
choose	chose	chosen
freeze	froze	frozen
speak	spoke	spoken
steal	stole	stolen
weave	wove	woven

do	did	done
fly	flew	flown
go	went	gone
lie	lay	lain
see	saw	seen

swear	swore	sworn
tear	tore	torn
wear	wore	worn

drink	drank	drunk
ring	rang	rung
shrink	shrank	shrunk
sing	sang	sung
sink	sank	sunk
spring	sprang	sprung
stink	stank	stunk
swim	swam	swum

blow	blew	blown
draw	drew	drawn
grow	grew	grown
know	knew	known
throw	threw	thrown

eat	ate	eaten
fall	fell	fallen
give	gave	given
shake	shook	shaken
take	took	taken

ride	rode	ridden
rise	rose	risen
write	wrote	written

bite	bit	bitten
hide	hid	hidden

4. The present tense and past participle are the same, but the past tense is different.

become	became	become
come	came	come
run	ran	run

16.7 In a conversation circle, ask:

What have you done that you really enjoyed doing?

16.8 Test students' mastery of use of the present perfect tense.

Written Test Idea

Write about what you have done that you enjoyed doing.

Oral Test Idea

Prepare a brief talk on things you have done or not done, seen or not seen. Model:

> **I have seen the moon. I haven't been to the moon. I have seen a rainbow at sunset. I have seen the northern lights. I haven't gone to the North Pole. I have watched a hockey game. I haven't skated.**

Topic 17   "What has made you the way you are?"

> *Contrast of present and past tenses: simple past, present perfect, past continuous, and "used to"*

17.1 Contrast the present and past tense: present perfect (indefinite), simple past (definite), past progressive (continuing), and **used to** (extended over a period of time or repeated). Write the following questions on the board and have the students interview you first, as a model, and then each other:

Indefinite question:

> **What has someone given you that pleased you?**

Definite answer:

> **(Stacey gave me a ring .)**

> **What have you given someone that pleased him or her?**
>
> **Who has helped you and how did you feel?**
>
> **Whom have you helped and how did you feel?**
>
> **Have you done something to protect someone or some animal? What was he/she/it doing at the time?**
>
> **What do you like to do?**
>
> **What did you like to do when you were younger?**

17.2 Use diagrams to contrast the verb forms used to describe past time. Give students copies of Reproduction Page 36, **"Verbs in the Past."**

REPRODUCTION PAGE 36

CHAPTER 2, ACTIVITY 17.2

VERBS IN THE PAST

Fill in the appropriate blanks.

Present perfect: something that has happened at some indefinite period in the past, any time up to the present moment.

	(red)	(blue)	(red)	(yellow)	(orange)	(green)
Yes		I	've		eaten	fish.
		I	have		played	volley ball.
?	Have	I			eaten	bean sprouts?
	Haven't	I			played	tennis?
No		I	have	n't		
		I	have	not		

Simple past: something that happened at a specific past time.

Yes						caught	a fish.
		I					
?	Did	I					
No							

Past progressive: an incomplete activity or series of acts in the past.

Yes						writing	a letter.
		I	was				
?							
No							

17.3 How do we spend our time? All of you answer the following questions about how you think you spend your time each day. Write the questions on the board and have students write their answers on a sheet of paper.

> **How many hours do you spend in classes?**
> **How much time do you spend talking with friends?**
> **How long do you talk on the phone?**
> **How much time do you spend getting yourself ready for school?**
> **How much time do you spend studying?**
> **How much time do spend watching television?**
> **How much time do you spend reading?**
> **How many hours a day do you spend working?**
> **How much time do you spend sleeping?**

Collect their papers. Ask them to keep daily diaries of actual time spent for the week. Then have them compare their diaries with their original estimates. Model record:

11:00 P.M.–6:30 A.M.	7½ hrs.	I slept from eleven thirty until six thirty.
6:30 A.M.–7:00 A.M.	½ hr.	I got up at six thirty and was dressed by seven.
7:00 A.M.–7:15 A.M.	¼ hr.	I ate breakfast from seven to seven fifteen.

At the end of the week add the total time spent in each activity during the week, calculate the average time spent on each activity during a day, compare the hours actually spent in each activity with the estimates made the week before. Return the papers and the estimates. Model:

> **I said that I spent ___1___ hour(s) ___studying___ , but I actually spent an average of ___1½___ hours.**

Share your diary with a partner and answer this question:

> **What did you find out that surprised you?**

Share with the whole group something that each of you found out about yourself or your partner.

17.4 In groups of three or four, talk about your grandparents. Give students copies of Reproduction Page 37, **"Grandparents,"** to use as a guide for this conversation.

REPRODUCTION PAGE 37

CHAPTER 2, ACTIVITY 17.4

GRANDPARENTS

1. Are your grandparents living?

2. Where do they or did they live?

3. Did they always live there? If not, where did they live before?

4. What language did they speak when they were children?

5. What languages did they learn?

6. What kind of work did they do?

7. What kind of interesting things have they done?

8. To which of your grandparents do or did you feel closest?

9. Have you spent much time with your grandparents?

10. How much influence have they had on your life?

17.5 To provide a model, write a composition of several paragraphs about your own grandparents, organizing the details around the questions in each of the groups on Reproduction Page 38 used in Activity 17.4. Give students copies of your composition to read and use as a model for compositions about their grandparents.

17.6 In groups of three or four, talk about things you have done, with the following questions on the board as a guide. If you are not in too great demand as a resource person, join a group as an active participant:

> **When you were a child, what did you do to get what you wanted?**
>
> **Have you done the same thing recently?**
>
> **When you were a child, how did you avoid doing what you didn't want to do? Did you refuse? Get mad? Ignore it? Go away? Have you done the same thing recently?**
>
> **Have you ever wanted to do something but decided not to do it? What was it? Why did you decide not to do it?**

17.7 In a conversation circle, ask:

> **What did you used to do often but seldom do any more?**

Recall each other's answers:

> **__Carlos__ , you used to _____ .**

Then ask:

What do you do now that you couldn't do as a child?

17.8 Give each student a copy of the worksheet from Reproduction Page 38, **"Am I Creative?"** Read the questions in class to make sure the students understand them, then ask them to answer the questions at home for discussion in small groups the next day. Collect their worksheets when they are finished and make notes of their answers to the last question to use later in Activity 18.1.

REPRODUCTION PAGE 38

CHAPTER 2, ACTIVITY 17.8

AM I CREATIVE?

1. Within the last six months, have you tried anything different? Have you made any change in your relationship with anyone? Have you made anything? Have you had a new idea?

2. Can you think of any experience in your childhood that has helped you try new things? Can you think of any experience that made you believe you can't do certain things?

3. Has there been anyone who encouraged you to do new things or who discouraged you from doing new things?

4. What are you going to do different this month or this year?

5. Can you think of something you have accomplished that was difficult?

17.9 Write a model composition, with a paragraph based on each question in activity 17.8. Give students copies of it to read and have them write similar compositions.

17.10 Test students' use of verb tenses.

Written Test Idea

Write a paragraph describing what was for you a happy time when you were younger.

Oral Test Idea

Think back two years and prepare a one-minute talk describing yourself then and what you had, what you wanted, how you've changed, or how you've stayed the same.

Topic 18 "What would you do?"

The conditional

18.1 Teach the conditional as the future of the past, referring to students' worksheets of Reproduction Page 38, **"Am I Creative?"** Look at the answers to the last question on that sheet and ask:

Who said that he or she would _____ ?

Continue until you have asked about each student's answer to that question.

18.2 Draw a long line on the board or on a strip of paper along one side of the room, to represent a time continuum and demonstrate the tenses in answer to the following question:

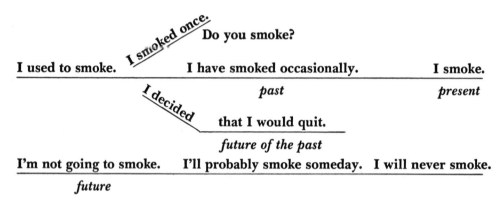

Initial your position on the line and have students initial theirs.

18.3 Demonstrate use of the conditional **would** in contrary-to-fact statements. (In English, the subjunctive form **were** is correct with singular subjects in conditional sentences that are contrary to fact but **was** is used widely.)

> **I'm not an animal. If I were, I would want to be a squirrel.**
> **I'm not a doctor. If I were, I would like to be a psychiatrist.**
> **If I were president, I would solve the energy problem.**
> **I'm not an elected official. If I were, I would like to be a senator.**

Repeat these sentences aloud and write them on the board. Have students form groups of three, and have each group think of similar statements and write them on the board.

18.4 Have students complete these sentences and choose one to share with the entire class:

> **If I were my mom or dad, _____ .**
> **If I were the teacher of this class, _____ .**
> **If I were the director of this school, _____ .**
> **If I were the president of the United States, _____ .**

18.5 Give each student a copy of the worksheet from Reproduction Page 39, **"What Would You Do?"** Read the questions aloud and pause for students to write their answers. Have them read the questions again silently and note down how they think their mother and father would answer. In small groups, discuss their reactions and make up a similar question to ask the teacher or another student when the whole class meets together.

18.6 In groups of five, ask students to choose one of these tasks as a project for the group:

> **If all of you together were building a dream house, what would it be like?**

If you could plan a school, what would it be like?

Make drawings or any kind of presentation that you would like to show to the class.

REPRODUCTION PAGE 39

CHAPTER 2, ACTIVITY 18.5

WHAT WOULD YOU DO?

	Would your parents do the same?	
	Mother	Father
1. If you were driving at night and saw someone in trouble, what would you do?		
2. If a friend gave you the answers for an exam, what would you do?		
3. If a teacher gave you a zero on an exam, accusing you unjustly of having cheated, what would you do?		
4. If you bought something and found it defective when you got home, what would you do?		
5. If you had a million dollars, what kind of house would you have?		
6. If the government chose you to go to another planet, would you go?		
7. If you had graduated from high school last year, would you be studying at a university now?		
8. If someone were to give you a scholarship to go to a particular university but you didn't like the university, would you accept the scholarship and would you go?		
9. If you could be successful at one thing, what would you do?		
10. If you found out tonight that you were going to move to another city, how would you feel?		

18.7 Contrast **hope** (for something that is possible or has some chance of happening) with **wish** (uncertainty about the future, or contrary to fact). In small groups share your answers to these questions:

What do you hope that you can do?

What do you wish that you could do?

What do you hope that someone will do?

What do you wish that someone would do?

What do you wish that you had done?

18.8 Write a model composition answering the questions:

What do you wish that you had done this year?

Would it have changed anything if you had done it?

Give students a copy of your paragraph to read and use as a model for similar compositions. Now, repeat the exercise, looking into the future:

> **What do you hope you will do next year?**
>
> **What do you wish you could do next year?**

18.9 Test students' mastery of the conditional.

Written Test Idea

Complete these sentences:

> **If I had my own car,** _____.
>
> **If I were five years older,** _____.
>
> **If I had a gun,** _____.
>
> **If I could do it again,** _____.
>
> **If I knew why,** _____.
>
> **If I had my driver's license,** _____.
>
> **If I didn't have any money,** _____.
>
> **If I were my mom or dad,** _____.
>
> **If I had a lot of money,** _____.

Oral Test Idea

Plan a one-minute talk about how you would live if you were living alone right now, answering these questions:

> **What are several things that you would do that you don't do now?**
>
> **What are several things that you would continue to do in the same way as you are doing now?**

Topic 19 "What are you looking forward to?"

Two- and three-word verbs (phrasal and prepositional verbs)

19.1 Help students understand two- and three-word verbs such as **cut down, find out, look at, put up with.** Play the tape-recorded song from the Longman cassette, "I'm Looking Forward to the Day."

> 1. I'm *looking forward* to the day
>   When everybody can stand and say:
>   You can't *get away with* that!
>   If you *take out,* you must *put back,*
>   Help us to save our skies and seas
>   And don't let them *cut down* all our trees.

Chorus:

> So *listen to* their words and *look at* their faces,
> Are they going to *wipe out* our wide open spaces?
> *Think about* the noise you have to *put up with,*
> Is this the way you want your children to live?

   2. It's time to *stand up for* what you feel,
     To *make sure* that what they say is real.
     Find out what they really mean
     Is it what you have often seen?
     What they invent *turns out* to be
     The ruin of our society.

   3. I'm *looking forward to* the day
     When I see the clouds all *roll away*.
     If the aeroplanes don't fly
     We can *make out* the blue in the sky.
     Let's live the simple life again
     And learn to *get on with* other men. *

Write the words of the song on the board, leaving blank spaces for the two- and three-word verbs italicized in the lyrics above. As you play the tape-recorded song, let different students write in the missing words.

19.2 Look at the underlined two- and three-word verbs and help the students make up some personal questions with them. Write the questions on the board as they think of them. Then form groups of three or four to ask each other the questions.

19.3 Have the students who are interested in word study listen again to the song, "I'm Looking Forward to the Day," and try to think of single verbs synonymous for some of the two- and three-word verbs. Ask the students if the single word conveys a different feeling from the two- or three-word equivalent?

19.4 Identify which of the two- and three-word verbs must be separated in order to add an object pronoun. For example, these two-word verbs are separable:

     If you *take out*
     Take it *out.*
     You must *put back*
     Put it *back.*

These two-word verbs are inseparable:

     Listen to their words
     Listen it to
     Think about the noise
     Think it about

Have the students make a copy of the lyrics and circle the separable two-word verbs.

19.5 In a conversation circle ask:

     What are you looking forward to?

---

*Ken Wilson and Keith Morrow, "I'm Looking Forward to the Day," *Goodbye Rainbow, Songs for Students of English as a Foreign Language.* Longman, 1975.

ASSESSING ACHIEVEMENT OF OBJECTIVES

Final Written Evaluation Ideas

Write a composition about yourself, using these questions as a guide.

Present

> Who are you?
> What kind of a person are you? What are you like?
> How old are you?
> What do you do?
> What do you like to do?
> What do you do well?
> What makes you happy?
> What bothers you or makes you angry?
> Do you believe that you can be successful at something?
> Do you believe in a life after death?

Past

> What were you like when you were a child?
> Where did you live?
> Did you have a pet?
> Who did you play with? What did you play?
> What was your favorite holiday? How did you celebrate it?
> When did you learn to ride a bicycle?
> Have you ever ridden horseback? Where and when did you ride horseback the first time?
> When did you first fall in love?
> Where did you start school? Did you like it? Did your teacher make you feel good?
> Have you traveled much?
> Have you read much? Have you read something that has had much influence on your thinking?
> Have you changed much in your ideas? Has someone had much influence on your ideas?
> From whom or what have you learned a lot?
> What did your mother used to tell you to do? How did you feel?
> What did your father used to tell you to do?
> What did you used to beg them to do? How did they feel?
> What did people tell you to do?
> What did you tell other people to do?

Future and Conditional

What are you going to do tonight? What would you like to do tonight?

What will you do when you finish school?

What would you be doing now if you had already finished school?

What are you going to do next summer? What would you do if you could?

What do you want to do someday?

What would you do if you had lots of money?

Final Oral Evaluation Idea

Present a three-minute talk based on the questions above. Record the talk, listen to it, and note any errors that you find. Answer these questions:

Are you satisfied with your work and what you have learned in this class?

What would you have to do to feel satisfied?

Do you need or want any help from your teacher?

Resources

Here is a list of selected resources that are valuable for the classroom library or as student texts. Addresses of publishers and distributors are listed in Appendix A.

Text Materials

Adult English One (also Two and Three) by John Chapman. Paperbound. Prentice-Hall, 1978. Interesting texts about real people and activities. Good presentation of grammar with structure tables. Past tense introduced very early. Treats separable and inseparable two-part verbs. Practical and stimulating for high school students and adults.

American English by the Audio-Visual Method. Didier International. Heinle & Heinle Enterprises. Filmstrips and taped dialogs for use with the question-answer technique (see Chapter 1, Audiovisual Method). Highly recommended.

American Kernel Lessons: Intermediate by Robert O'Neil et al. Paperbound. Longman, 1978. A review grammar with interesting, illustrated situations to help students ask and answer questions. Includes a serial story with an episode in each lesson. Recommended for getting students involved in talking and reading.

Check the Deck. Teachers' Collaborative, 1978. Eight decks of fifty-two cards each. Each deck has thirteen questions, each question has four answers. Illustrated by drawings. Variety of games can be played while practicing using nouns and verbs in various tenses. Recommended.

Dyad Learning Program. Verb Choices and Verb Forms, Prepositions, and Pronouns and Determiners by Alice C. Pack. Paperbound. Newbury House, Publishers, 1977. Three volumes. Exercises with an intriguing format. Attractive books. Modern, mature, useful vocabulary. Students work in pairs, one with a student's book and the other with a tutor's book (actually the same book turned upside down). The student's book has blanks to be filled in, while the tutor's book has the correct answers.

Elementary Course in English by Willard D. Sheeler. Paperbound. English Language Services, 1971 Can be used as textbook-workbook. Units organized around grammar topics, which are introduced by means of clear, easily understood diagrams. Short readings make good models for students to write brief compositions about themselves. Recommended.

English by Objectives by Nicolas Ferguson and Maire O'Reilly. Evans Brothers. Filmstrips and taped dialogs. Exercises in writing and reading. Focuses on performance objectives rather than grammar objectives. Well worth considering even though the orientation is British.

English for a Changing World by Ronald Wardhaugh et al. Paperbound. Scott, Foresman and Company, 1976. Four books and workbooks. Very well-illustrated dialogs and exercises. Excellent presentation of grammar concepts. Good grammar progression with past tense introduced in the first book.

Goodbye Rainbow, Songs for Students of English as a Foreign Language by Ken Wilson and Keith Morrow. Paperbound. Longman, 1975. Songs using advanced grammar concepts. Controversial themes are good conversation starters for mature students. With cassette.

InterCom: English for International Communication Levels, Beginning to Advanced. Books 1–6 by Richard C. Yorkey et al. Paperbound. Litton Educational Publishing International, 1977. Attractive modern, mature, useful vocabulary. Short, well-illustrated dialogs. Exercises in context. Lively listening component with good voices and music on cassettes. Stimulating book for student use. On the negative side: little affective content, grammar poorly organized.

Jazz Chants: Rhythms of American English for Students of English as a Second Language by Carolyn Graham. Paperbound. Oxford University Press, 1978. Catchy poetry. Quick rhythmic chants, very well recorded on tape cassette. Follows a good beginning grammar sequence. Excellent for use with audiovisual techniques. Highly recommended.

Learning American English by Grant Taylor. Paperbound. McGraw-Hill Book Company, 1956. Good workbook. Very good, simple grammar explanation with each topic. Excellent graphic contrast of statements, questions, and negatives. Unfortunately no high-interest content, but still recommended.

Mister Monday & Other Songs for the Teaching of English by Ken Wilson. Paperbound. Longman, 1972. With a recording on cassette of lively music and lyrics, some of these "grammar" songs are excellent for teaching and fun. For mature students.

New Horizons in English by Lars Mellgren and Michael Walker. Paperbound. Addison-Wesley Publishing Company, 1973. Six small volumes. Well illustrated with colored drawings for meaning. Good sequence for introducing basic grammar structures which are simply stated in tabular form in each lesson. Recommended for student use but not for classroom activity.

Progressive Picture Compositions Pupils' Book by Doun Byrne. Paperbound. Longman, 1967. Sequences of four story-telling pictures with exercises to help tell the stories. Pictures could be reproduced on transparencies and used with the audiovisual method (see Chapter 1, Audiovisual Method). Recommended.

Talk It over: Discussion Topics for Intermediate Students by L. G. Alexander et al. Paperbound. Longman, 1978. Thirty situations established by dialogs or pictures to stimulate the pros and cons and get students involved in discussion. Recommended.

Writing

Now Poetry edited by Charles L. Cutler et al. Paperbound booklet. Xerox Education Publications, 1975. Intriguing little book of poetry patterns and ideas. Recommended.

Writing Errors You Hate to Make and How to Avoid Them. Paperbound booklet. Xerox Education Publications, 1976. Fun book to help you find mistakes in punctuation, subject and verb agreement, pronouns and antecedents.

Readers

American Topics: A Reading-Vocabulary Text for Speakers of English as a Second Language by Robert C. Lugton. Paperbound. Prentice-Hall, 1978. Interesting topics for mature high school students or adults with considerable competence and the motivation to improve their skills.

Detailed exercises for individual or small-group work. Relevant, involving discussion questions.

Evans Graded Verse 1, 2, 3 by Michael Knight and Ronald Ridout. Paperbound. Evans Brothers, 1977. Songs, rhymes, and poems for students of English. Pleasant, light-hearted little books.

Forestville Tales: International Folk Stories by Aaron Berman. Macmillan, 1978. Eight stories to read and tell. Illustrations in sequence to aid understanding and storytelling.

Getting into It . . . An Unfinished Book by Dave Blot and Phyllis Berman Sher. Paperbound. Language Innovations, 1978. True-to-life stories, based on the problems and feelings of students of English in a large, American city. Highly recommended for involving students in open discussion.

Longman Structural Readers. Paperbound. Longman, 1975. Excellent graded readers.

New Method Supplementary Readers. Paperbound, Longman, 1976. Abridged novels, beautifully done to keep the flavor and language of the original. Highly recommended.

Open-ended Stories by Milton Velder and Edwin Cohen. Paperbound. Globe Book Co. 1973. Twenty incomplete stories to get students involved. Relevant to high school students.

Point 31 Magazine—Vols. 1, 2, 3. Paperbound, magazine format. Reader's Digest, 1978. Variety of short articles and stories with topics and language to appeal to high school students. Intermediate to advanced.

Reading and Exercise Series edited by Willard D. Sheeler. Paperbound. English Language Services, 1975. Six, graded readers, incorporating original stories from and adaptations of the classics. Stories contain suprise and feeling to stimulate interest in reading and talking. Especially good for high school and adult students.

Real Life Reading Skills by Beatrice Jackson Levin. Paperbound. Scholastic Book Services, 1977. A practical book, designed to develop functional reading skills: signs and labels, directions, forms and applications, reference material, newspapers, consumer education. Highly recommended. Clear, direct style.

Literature

Animal Farm by George Orwell. Paperbound. The New American Library. This allegory—the well-intentioned, apparently democratic takeover of the farm by the animals, with subsequent abuse of power resulting in a completely totalitarian regime—is universal in time and place. It brings up questions of how free we can be and what we have to give up to make freedom as real as possible.

The Diary of Anne Frank, dramatization by Frances Goodrich and Albert Hackett. Paperbound. Dramatists Play Service. A sad, tragic play that also has humor warmth, beauty, pity, and hope.

Happy Journey to Camden & Trenton by Thornton Wilder. Paperbound. Dramatists Play Service. An excellent play that is loving and funny with good family dialogue.

Our Town by Thornton Wilder. Paperbound. Samuel French. A beautiful play that relates the story of life, love, and death in a small New England town.

The Pearl by John Steinbeck. Paperbound. Bantam Books. A fable that paints in sharp contrasts of black and white the problems of economic exploitation and the conflict between personal integrity and greed.

Seven Plays from American Literature. Paperbound. English Language Services. Short plays (about fifteen minutes each), adapted from short stories by famous American authors. Good for beginning to know and enjoy American literature. Recordings available. Excellent for taking parts and reading aloud.

Reference Grammars

Learning Grammar through Writing by Sandra M. Bell and James I. Wheeler. Paperbound. Educators Publishing Service, 1976. Reference grammar that is simply written and direct enough to be useful to beginners. Lists principal parts of irregular verbs, pronouns, prepositions, and conjunctions. Gives models of letters. Explains elements of sentences, paragraphs, and compositions. Recommended.

Dictionaries

Webster's New World Dictionary of the American Language. Paperbound. Popular Library, 1973. Concise definitions, easy to understand. Parts of speech, plural forms, past tense, and participles. Clear pronunciation key. Highly recommended for students.

Classroom Library

A Handbook of English Grammar: Seventh Edition by R. W. Zandvoort. Hardbound. Longman. Old-fashioned and reliable. Useful for quick reference by the teacher and also for advanced students. Interesting for browsing, especially section on word formation and derivation.

A Reference Grammar for Students of English by R. A. Close. Paperbound. Longman, 1975. Modern and interesting interpretation of grammar by a man with forty years experience teaching English in many countries. For teachers and advanced students.

Common Errors in English and How to Avoid Them by Alexander M. Witherspoon. Paperbound. Littlefield, Adams and Company, 1973. Lists words and phrases frequently misused, explain correct usage. Guide to correct pronunciation and spelling. Useful for intermediate and advanced students.

Voice and Diction: Applied Phonation and Phonology by John W. Black and Ruth B. Irwin. Hardbound. Charles E. Merrill Publishing Company, 1969. Detailed analysis of English vowels and consonants. Very readable. Interesting exercises for awareness and correction.

For Teachers

Communication Starters and Other Activities for the ESL Classroom by Judy E. Winn-Bell Olsen. Unbound, loose-leaf. The Alemany Press, 1977. Great variety, including excellent map activities for partners and small groups, references for finding pictures, instructions for making visual aids, a sequence of lessons for teaching grammar concepts with Cuisenaire Rods. Recommended.

English in Three Acts by Richard G. Via. Paperbound. The University Press of Hawaii, 1976. Delightful book from a man who loves drama and appreciates people or vice versa. Convinces you to try to produce a play with intermediate students and shows you how to make it an exciting, profitable experience. The activities used to teach actors are equally useful for teaching speakers of English as a second language. The seven one-act plays are excellent for reading out loud. Epilogue includes an invaluable annotated list of plays suitable for English language learners. Most highly recommended.

3

Beyond the Beginning

To maintain enthusiasm and interaction in the classes as well as provide opportunity for academic growth is a challenge for teachers of language beyond the beginning level. In this chapter we give suggestions and describe activities that expose students to literature and that help them learn about other cultures, review grammar, and practice writing and speaking on an advanced level.

INVOLVING STUDENTS IN CURRICULUM DEVELOPMENT

The easiest way to achieve relevance in language learning is to give students an opportunity to develop a curriculum based on their interests. The trick is to involve students in creating a curriculum and then to relate the new curriculum to your course objectives. Students and teachers can work together, first to discover areas of interest and then to develop minicourses, or units, based on those interests. To accomplish this goal is easier than it sounds, and highly rewarding.

Involving students in the creation of a miniunit assures its relevance since it is developed from the students' own needs. We use a process, developed by Leland W. Howe and Mary Martha Howe (the book is described in the resources section), which is fun and liberating for students and teacher. This process allows for creativity and encourages nonjudgmental response as well. Developing the curriculum is as meaningful a learning experience as the curriculum itself, perhaps even more so. Students create options, make decisions, and deal with their own values.

Example of a Curriculum Development Process

Objective: To learn a process for decision making and create a relevant and enriching unit of study.

1. *Make a list of topics by brainstorming.* Ask students what topics and problems they would like to study. Write the ideas on the board so everyone can see the growing list. Don't forget to add your own ideas. Students can think of topics such as these:

clothes	diets
drugs	peers
grades	cars
pets	sports
gossip	what's acceptable
sex	parents
future	death
friends	astrology
themselves	authority
their bodies	independence
smoking	television
medium (spiritualism)	religion
parties	God
school	love
dates	

2. *Choose a topic.* Ask students to look at the list and choose a topic they would like to investigate. Use the following questions as criteria to help them decide on a topic:

- **Does it interest most of us?**
- **Will it help us learn about ourselves—goals, values, our effect on others?**
- **Will it help us learn about other people and the world?**
- **Can we get enough information?**
- **Do we feel comfortable with the topic?**
- **Will it help develop the skills of thinking and problem solving?**
- **Will it help develop the foreign language skills of reading, writing, and speaking?**

3. *Divide the topic into subtopics.* Ask students what ideas they think of in relation to the topic and list them on a wall chart, a flip chart, or on the board. Encourage imaginations to run free. Don't stop the flow with comments and critiques. Don't worry about order, organization, or appropriateness at this step. This kind of free association helps to give teacher and students a sense of being creative and involved. One class listed these ideas on **independence**:

freedom	curfews
restrictions	parents
teenagers	minimum age
adults	drinking
teenagers from other countries	dating
sex	peer pressure
responsibilities	peers
support	money
friends	budgeting
around the world	me
independent movements	writers
jobs	school
driving	punishments
no rules	

Next, have the class examine the list for similarities and group the ideas in natural categories.

me	dating	freedom
school	drinking	writers
teenagers from other countries	sex	no rules
teenagers	driving	around the world
peers	budgeting	responsibilities
friends	money	independent movements
support	jobs	restrictions
peer pressure	parents	punishment
	adults	curfews
		minimum age

4. *Develop questions about the subtopic.* Help students focus on what they want to know or what they want to say. Form small groups. Have each group choose a subtopic and make a list of questions about it. One class developed these questions on the subtopic **freedom:**

- **How free am I?**
- **How do I claim independence in my life?**
- **Where am I functioning independently, and in what areas am I independent of others?**
- **What are some of the risks of being too independent?**
- **What are the trade-offs in being independent?**
- **At what age does independence cease to be a problem?**
- **How independent would I really like to be? Independent of family? Independent of the whole world? Alone?**
- **How independent would I be if I were of a different race?**
- **What would happen if we were all independent?**

5. *Develop activities from the questions.* Have students group themselves in pairs. Have each pair choose a question from the group of questions and develop an activity or project idea that is related to the question. Teachers must involve themselves with the students at this time in order to help create meaningful and lively activities that involve more than reading and writing. Activities will be more fun to do and more meaningful for the students if:

- students make value judgments;
- students solve problems;
- activities involve the senses;
- activities give students a chance to create something;
- activities help students to fantasize, role play, and try out new behaviors;
- activities further develop students' skills in at least one area of the foreign language.

A group of Spanish students presented one activity in the following manner:

Question: **What kind of independence do others have?**

Activity: Create an interview based on questions that will help you find out about customs of people from different countries and backgrounds. Foreign-born teenagers, exchange students, immigrant families, students from other communities, and students in your own school are a good source. Sample questions.

What is expected of you by your parents and relatives?
When are you expected to work?
When are you expected to contribute to your own support?
Where do grandparents live when they can no longer live alone?

Share the answers with the whole class in order to compare value systems:

Who does the same things you do?
What was different that surprised you?

6. *Make the activities satisfy the objectives of the unit.* Trying to think up activities based on objectives is apt to be sterile and get in the way of the creative process. So at this point, after they have created interesting activities, ask the students to think about what they want to accomplish as a result of having studied this unit. The teacher shares what he or she wants to achieve and then coordinates student objectives with teacher objectives by making a chart, listing the activities on the side and the unit objectives across the top to see how they

mesh (see the sample chart). If there are some blanks in the chart (objectives not being met), you can suggest that students revise some activities to fill the voids. Ask questions like:

- **How could we change an activity from writing to doing something?**
- **Do you see any activity that might involve reading?**

7. *Decide how to teach the unit.* Ask the following questions to get students' input so that you can plan a structure that will facilitate the teaching and learning of the unit:

- **What classroom organization will be best for this unit: learning centers, individual study areas, meeting outside the classroom?**
- **What requirements should there be for the unit: journals, collages, reading selective literature, creating and conducting an interview?**
- **What methods of evaluation will be used: learning contracts, student evaluation, conferences, rating scales?**

8. *Implement the unit.* Have students help choose the order of the activities. Let them provide leadership and help determine the size and makeup of groups for each activity.

To give a sense of closure, we have found it enjoyable and meaningful to end units with a celebration activity, such as cooking and eating together, going to a restaurant, having a folk dance, acting out a play, or creating a sports event based on another culture.

9. *Evaluate the unit.* The following questions will help to evaluate the unit. Both students and teacher need to be heard:

- **Was there active participation by a majority of the students?**
- **How meaningful were the activities?**
- **Was there a lot of interest and enthusiasm maintained?**
- **What were the high points?**
- **What were the low points?**
- **If I could teach/study this unit again, what would I do differently?**
- **I enjoyed most _____ .**
- **The most meaningful thing for me was _____ .**
- **The least interesting thing to me was _____ .**

Objectives

Activities	Reading and Literature	Writing	Awareness of Self and Others	Communication Skills	Vocabulary Development	Grammar Review
Drawing a series of continuums defining areas of independence			X	X	X	X
Conducting an interview to find out about others			X	X	X	X
Reading *The Little Prince*	X		X		X	
Writing an essay fantasizing how independent the student would like to be		X	X	X	X	X
Celebrating another country's independence day	X		X	X		

EXAMINING ALTERNATIVES TO A REGULAR CLASS PERIOD

How many minutes a day does your class meet? How many days a week? Who decided that? Does it really have to be that way? Is there some reason for doing it differently?

When we stop to consider such questions and look for options, we find some really exciting alternatives:

1. Bilingual, or immersion, programs in which students study mathematics, history, and other subjects for a prescribed period of time each day in the foreign language.
2. Programs of minicourses that give students opportunities to try out learning a language or to develop special interests using the language.
3. Intensive classes that meet for several hours a day, which give students the chance to learn enough language to be able to communicate quickly.

Bilingual programs have become common in elementary schools. Bilingual programs in secondary schools are worth more consideration because students can learn the foreign language faster as well as satisfy other course requirements. To try a bilingual program may require little more than the language teacher's being certified to teach another subject, or the social studies teacher's being fluent in a foreign language. There are schools that are developing such programs. Alternatives to regular language classes include: minicourses in music, art, cooking, crafts, culture, and even human relations; specialized vocational programs to equip students for bilingual positions in medicine, police work, tourist industry, business and foreign trade, government; and intensive language teaching programs.

Maintaining such a program requires energy and commitment on the part of everyone involved: the students, the parents, the faculty, the administration, and the community. It all seems worthwhile, however, when we see how the students value the program:

"I have learned more about myself and other people during these classes and trip than I have during my 13 years of school."

"Getting along with and learning to appreciate the people in this class has been the most important preparation for me, not only for the trip, but for my life."

Example of an Intensive Class[1]

Objective: To stimulate greater interest in the foreign language, learn it faster, and use it in natural social interactions.

Kenston High School offers students who have completed one year of high school foreign language study an intensive Spanish or French class as an alternative to regular class. The intensive class meets for two and a half hours a day from September to December and culminates, during the first three weeks in December, in a homestay experience in a foreign country.

The extended learning period of two and a half hours a day allows the class to become immersed in the language without the usual time wasted in beginning and ending a class period every forty minutes. Field trips and other activities are possible. The class is able to go to students' homes to study, to eat together, to go to museums, to go to other communities, or to go to local colleges. During this longer time together, the students use the language in a natural, lively way. They learn idiomatic expressions while they eat, how to talk about what they see and like in someone's house, how to ask about and talk to pets, and, generally, to speak about everyday things. While driving to and from students' homes and other places, they learn how to give and take directions, to discuss what they did at school or at the museum, and so on.

The class spends a lot of time learning to work together, listening to each other, sharing thoughts and experiences, and generally learning to accept each other. They do this in their new language, using the many activities suggested in this book. They use the curriculum development process described earlier in this chapter to create units of study. We find an unbelievable amount of informal learning takes place in this environment in addition to learning that takes place through structured teaching.

The intensive class is in itself an exciting concept and can be set up at any school even without its culmination in a foreign trip. The program at Kenston, however, climaxes with a three-week homestay in a foreign country. Teachers arrange for transportation to the foreign country, and The Experiment in International Living (see the resources, page 124) arranges for the homestay. While in the foreign country, each student lives with a family, usually in a small community where little or no English is spoken. The student's task is, of course, to speak the foreign language, but more important, to adapt to a new culture—an eye-opening, mind-stretching experience. The unique aspect of the trip is that it is not a vacation, but an educational experience on school time. We feel that the walls of the classroom need to be opened to allow for real-world education to be a part of learning.

Because students live with families in the country of their target language, the trip costs little more than transportation. Since this travel experience has become an established part of the foreign language program at Kenston, most of the students who want to, somehow find money to go—even though Kenston is a diverse community, and many of our students' families have limited incomes. Some students begin to plan and save money in junior high school.

1. Beverly Wattenmaker, "An Intensive Approach to High School Foreign Language Learning," *Foreign Language Annals*, Vol. 12, No. 1 (February, 1979). Publisher of *Foreign Language Annals* is American Council on the Teaching of Foreign Languages, Inc., 2 Park Avenue, New York, N.Y. 10016.

INVOLVING STUDENTS WITH LITERATURE

Reading foreign literature can be an enriching experience and certainly a skill to develop and an activity to be encouraged. Foreign language teachers remember the thrill they felt when they, for the first time, read a novel, poem, or classic work in the foreign language, and they are anxious to have their students experience the same joy. Unfortunately, when literature is introduced too early in the student's foreign language study, it can be a frustrating and negative experience. Students need to have a good understanding of basic language structure and an adequate vocabulary. And they also need to have some interest in the material and some desire to read it. We have found that relating what we are reading to the students' own lives provides motivation and increases understanding. We begin with plays, novels, readings, stories, and poetry of simple language and everyday concerns such as those listed under literature at the end of the language chapters.

Reading good literature is an excellent way for students to learn skills of decision making, problem solving, and conflict resolution. Being able to understand the situations in which characters in a play or novel are involved is a first step toward understanding our own situations. Recognizing the cause and effect of conflict in a story we have just read can help us learn to recognize some of our own conflicts and think of options for resolving them. Analyzing risks that characters in a play have to face makes it easier for us to recognize what a risk is and decide whether or not we should face certain risks. Here are some ideas on how to get students involved in what they are reading.

Example of Personalizing Literature[2]

Objective: To enjoy literature, to learn skills of analysis and conflict resolution, and to make relevant application to our world today.

1. *Rank order*

- **Rank the characters in order of preference according to whom you would like to have as a friend/son/daughter/next door neighbor/teacher of your language class/roommate.**
- **On a scale of one to five, indicate whether the character makes you feel happy/sad/indifferent/angry/hostile. Rank several characters.**
- **What do you like about the work: style/characters/plot/ideas/setting? Rank order according to your personal preference.**
- **Which of the characters do you like? Rank them according to preference.**
- **Rank order the items on the following list according to how important you think each is for a character: friendship/love/money/security/family.**
- **If you had several hours of free time, would you play tennis/read another work by the same author/see a movie?**
- **Who would benefit most from reading this work: friends, parents, teachers, ministers?**

---

2. Adapted from Judith Acquario and Diane Birckbrichler, *A Personalized Approach to Teaching Literature at the Elementary School and Intermediate Levels of High School and College Instruction* (Ohio State University, unpublished).

2. *Continuum.* How would you/your parents/liberals/conservatives/prisoners evaluate the play or novel?

poor   *average*   *good*   *very good*   *excellent*

3. *Voting.* Do you agree or disagree?

If I were in _____'s situation, I would have acted the same way.

If I were stranded on a desert island, I would want _____ with me.

I know someone like _____ .

I find _____'s philosophy applicable to my life.

I have never felt like _____ did.

_____ reminded me of an experience in my childhood.

I would want to have someone like _____ as a friend.

The most tragic moment of the work was when _____ .

_____ is the most sensible character.

The ending means that human beings are essentially alone.

If I could go to see a play, _____ is one of the plays I would like to see.

A better ending would have been _____ .

The life of _____ can serve as a model for everyone.

4. *Incomplete sentences*

If I were in _____'s situation, I would _____ .

I admire _____ because _____ .

I prefer _____ because _____ .

I like the way _____ writes because _____ .

I would like to act the part of _____ because _____ .

The words of _____ make me feel _____ .

When _____, I felt sad.

When _____, I felt happy.

When _____, I felt confused.

When _____, I felt relieved.

When _____, I felt angry.

When _____, I felt involved.

The setting made me feel _____ .

The most tragic/most dramatic/happiest moment was _____ .

The work was/was not important to my life because _____ .

5. *Questions*

What sentence/word/passage do you remember from what you read last night?

What was your reaction to _____'s statement? If you had been the other character, what would you have said?

Did the character remind you of anyone you know?

What qualities do you have in common with _____ ?

How would you feel if you met _____ at a party?

Would you change the ending?

6. *What would you do?*

Imagine that you were to find youself in the same situation as _____ . What would be your reaction? How would you feel? What would you do?

If you were to meet one of the characters, what would you say? Prepare a list of statements and questions. Ask someone to play that person's role and respond to you.

You are one of the characters. Have some students ask you questions and you answer as you think that person would.

Imagine that you are one of the characters. Retell the story to another character in the book from your point of view.

Write a letter to one of the characters and have that person answer.

7. *Relating themes to your own life*

After you have finished reading the work and analyzing the characters and writing, the next step is to relate themes to the students' life. Have students help you think of themes from the work you have finished reading. Students reading St. Exupéry's *The Little Prince* thought of these themes which we will express here in English rather than French.

power	**search for meaning**
love	**friendship**
independence	**survival**
jealousy	**beauty**
loneliness	**adult**
concern for life	**child**

Then develop activities that help students reflect on these themes as they relate to their own lives. Here is one based on the theme of power from *The Little Prince*

Where do I have power?

In my family,

I don't have any power.	I have complete power over every one.

In my classes,

I don't have any power to enjoy myself.	I have total power to have a good time.

When I'm not in school,

I don't have any power to decide what I do.	I have complete freedom to decide.

Do you have the most power with your friends/in school/at home?

What are the things that you can decide for yourself?

In a conversation circle, ask:

What do you have in your purse or pants pocket that represents power? Will you share that with the group please? What is it and how does it represent power for you?

UNDERSTANDING OTHER CULTURES

We believe the language classroom should focus more on helping students understand and value cultural differences in general than on learning about the specific culture of one country. Learning culture from a book or movie has its place, but it becomes an intellectual and noninvolving exercise for most students. We find that making cultural differences come alive for students offers potential for self-growth as well as language growth. Creative teachers are generating fun and learning with Mexican dinners, German folk dances, French film festivals, and more.

Real-life cultural experiences add an extra dimension to foreign language learning. We find the following steps lead naturally to understanding and accepting people of other cultures and to wanting to be involved with someone or something different:

1. Developing self-awareness, with appreciation of our own strengths and some tolerance for our weaknesses.
2. Getting to know and accept the others around us—language class, team members, committees, family.
3. Reaching out to get involved with new people and new things in our culture.
4. And, finally, learning what people of other cultures think, believe, and value; and, by comparison, clarifying our own thoughts, beliefs and values.

The first two steps—knowing yourself and others—are the focus of the language class activity described in the preceding chapters. We find that when students have learned something about themselves and their own value system, they are more open to new and different ways. At this point, they are far more receptive to being involved in foreign (new) situations in which they have to use the human relations skills and language skills they have learned in the classroom.

Finding ways to involve students in foreign culture is easier than it might seem. We use a variety of resources not limited to the particular culture/language the students are studying. Our preparation and follow-up are in the target language, even though the experience may be in the student's native language. While an experience in the target language is preferable, the important part of the activity comes from the *differences in cultures.* Look around. Use students and friends to discover people and situations. Take advantage of whatever your community has to offer— relatives of students, business associates of a family, exchange students, an immigrant family, ethnic neighborhoods, foreign restaurants, nearby colleges with professors and families who speak a foreign language.

Once you pinpoint an activity, the students become involved through specific tasks. They need a structure to get the most out of what, for many, is their first experience with people who are "different."

1. If you are going to an ethnic restaurant, give an assignment to try new foods. Create some questions to ask the owners and waitresses or waiters if they are "foreign."

2. You can create a foreign experience on a strange street that is not part of your students' life. Ask students to observe and be prepared to describe what they see:

    Buildings?
    How many people on the street?
    Signs?
    What are the people doing?
    What is different about the people or shops?

3. If you go to meet a foreign family or visitor, have students prepare a list of questions ahead of time.

4. If you are fortunate enough to find an ethnic market or store that serves a different community, have students look for specifics.

    Who is shopping?

    What are the popular items being purchased?

    How are the vendors treating the customers?

    How is the food displayed?

    What is different about this shop and the ones students' families use?

    What is the specialty?

    How long have they been there?

    Where are the owners from?

    What language(s) do they speak?

We use the terms ethnic and foreign rather loosely to describe what has its origin in another country or what is simply something new and different. You can create a cultural experience going from a suburb to the inner city or to the country or vice versa, finding a Mexican or Italian restaurant, visiting an Amish community, or doing whatever seems different to your students. Visitors to colleges or industry provide a good source of subjects.

Once students begin to get involved with the ways other people do things, important changes take place: Students realize that there are other, perfectly natural and correct, ways of doing things; and they become more aware of their own value systems and discover that even with the differences they have much in common.

Of course, the very essence of culture is language—verbal, nonverbal, affective intonation. We are teaching culture every day when we teach students to communicate in a new language.

Resources

Here are some selected resources. Addresses of publishers and distributors are listed in Appendix A.

INVOLVING STUDENTS IN CURRICULUM DEVELOPMENT

The Cultural Revolution in Foreign Language Teaching: A Guide for Building the Modern Curriculum edited by Robert C. Lafayette. Paperbound. National Textbook Company, 1975. Selected papers from the 1975 Central States Conference of ACTFL (American Council of Teachers of Foreign Language) dealing with ways that language teachers, through their teaching, can contribute toward the acceptance of cultural pluralism. Presents good ideas to use in the classroom and interesting foreign language programs.

Miniguides: 16 Ready-made Mini-courses by the editors of *Scholastic Teacher.* Edited by Lois A. Markham and Patricia Fingeroth. Paperbound. Citation Press, 1975. Group of short courses that concentrate on a single, high-interest topic. Each course provides ideas for class activities and resources on the topic. Topics: the supernatural, sexual identity, loneliness and alienation, science fiction, death, survival, peace, humor. Helpful for teachers who wish to create units of study based on student interest.

"Personalizing the Curriculum," pages 364–371 of *Personalizing Education: Values Clarification and Beyond* by Leland W. Howe and Mary Martha Howe. Paperbound. Hart Publishing Company, 1975. Shows a process for developing curriculum to serve students' concerns. Highly recommended.

Teaching for Communication in the Foreign Language Classroom: A Guide for Building the Modern Curriculum edited by Renate A. Schulz. Paperbound. National Textbook Company, 1976. Selected papers from the 1976 Central State Conference of ACTFL (American Council of Teachers of Foreign Language). Of special note is the article "Strategies for Increasing Cross-Cultural Awareness" by Sidney L. Hahn.

EXAMINING ALTERNATIVES TO A REGULAR CLASS PERIOD

The Experiment for International Living. An organization that arranges foreign visits for cultural enrichment. Representatives in many countries make plans for groups or individuals to live with families and be involved with members of the community for fun and learning. We have used their help for the last seven years to arrange visits for some 300 students to Mexico, France, Canada, Guadaloupe, and Costa Rica.

Options and Perspectives: A Sourcebook of Innovative Foreign Language Programs in Action, K–12 by William D. Love and Lucille J. Honig. Paperbound. Modern Language Association, 1973. Discusses many successful innovative programs and alternative approaches to foreign-language teaching. Examples: immersion programs, individualized studies, vocation-oriented classes, summer language institutes, and short-term foreign language courses. Descriptions of the programs list schools and contact people so that the reader can follow through.

INVOLVING STUDENTS WITH LITERATURE

A Guidebook for Teaching Literature by Raymond J. Rodrigues and Dennis Badaczewski. Paperbound. Allyn and Bacon, 1978. Activities designed to involve students actively in the understanding and appreciation of literature.

UNDERSTANDING OTHER CULTURES

Cultural Awareness Workbooks by Barbara Oder et al., project directed by Stephan Ellenwood. Paperbound. The Wider Horizons Project, 1977. A series of workbooks for students who are traveling to Madrid, Mexico City, Paris, Munich, London, Rome, or Moscow. The exercises emphasize the development of cultural awareness (of the student's culture and other cultures). Excellent ideas for teachers' and students' activities before, during, and after their foreign stay. This unique approach, which involves students with the local people of another country, is exciting to teach and use.

Destination Germany and *Destination France.* Paperbound. Harrap and Company, 1976. The vocabulary and knowledge necessary for travel. Clever and interesting for planning an imaginary or real trip.

La Navidad by Agnes M. Brady and Margarita Marquez de Moats. *Noël* by R. de Roussy de Sales. *Weinacht* by Suzanne Ehrlich. Paperbound. National Textbook Company. Encylopedic collection of Christmas traditions and activities. Stories, songs, games, and history. Text that can be read by intermediate students. End vocabulary.

Modos de vivir: Invitación al mundo hispánico. Consultant: Zenia Sacks Da Silva. Macmillan, 1972. Series of filmstrips and tapes that can be used with a first-level Spanish course to introduce students to the richness and diversity of modern Spanish and Latin American cultures. The titles include "Panorama," "Vida hispánica," "Mercados y comidas," "Trabajos y diversiones," "Transportación," and "La fiesta brava."

Regional Dances of Mexico by Edith Johnston. *Zum Singen und Tanzen* by Elizabeth Schmidt. Paperbound. National Textbook Company. Songs and folk dances, with steps and music typical of different regions.

Scala Jugendmagazin. Distributor: Edelweiss Press. Magazine designed for students. Contains pictures, brief articles, poems, and interviews with young Germans. Deals with things that are important to young Germans either because they are engrossing activities or problems.

Scholastic Magazines. Scholastic Book Services. The German magazines, *Das Rad, Schuss,* and *Der Roller;* French magazines, *Bonjour, Ça va,* and *Chez nous;* and Spanish magazines *¿Qué tal?, El sol,* and *Hoy día* keep students up-to-date on current teenage dress and activities and give information on sports, cities, holidays, schools, homes. High school German teacher Nancy Germaine finds that the students often enjoy the magazine that is a level below their year in the language because it is then instantly enjoyable. The magazines' staffs will respond to letters in English or in the foreign language, which is a rewarding experience for the students.

Spanish Sign Language by G. J. Bawcutt, *French Sign Language* by M. R. Pearce, D. L. Ellis, *German Sign Language* by Robin Sawers. Paperbound. Harrap and Company, 1977. Photographs of road signs, store fronts, announcements, and other signs found in a city. Leading questions in English to help students decipher the signs. Recommended for small-group work.

Teaching Culture: Strategies for Foreign Language Educators by H. Ned Seilye. Paperbound. National Textbook Company. Practical suggestions for teaching students to discover cultural information rather than learn trivial "facts." Teaches students to ask the right questions.

Appendix A

ADDRESSES OF PUBLISHERS AND DISTRIBUTORS

Addison-Wesley Publishing Co., Inc.
Reading, Massachusetts 01867

The Alemany Press
Box 5265
San Francisco, California 94101

Allyn and Bacon, Inc.
470 Atlantic Avenue
Boston, Massachusetts 02210

Appleton-Century-Crofts
292 Madison Avenue
New York, New York 10017

Association for Supervision
    and Curriculum Development
1701 K Street, N.W.
Suite 1100
Washington, D.C. 20006

Bantam Books, Inc.
666 Fifth Avenue
New York, New York 10019

F. A. Brockhaus
Leberberg 25
6200 Wiesbaden, West Germany

CIDOC
Apdo. 479
Cuernavaca, Mexico

C-L/CLL
215 E. Chestnut Street, No. 1801
Chicago, Illinois 60611

Citation Press
906 Sylvan Avenue
Englewood Cliffs, New Jersey 07362

William Collins + World Publishing Co., Inc.
2080 West 117th Street
Cleveland, Ohio 44111

Confluent Education Development and Research
    Center
Box 30128
Santa Barbara, California 93105

The Continental Book Company
11-03 46th Avenue
Long Island City, New York 11101

Creative Resources Press
179 Spring Street
Saratoga Springs, New York 12866

Dell Publishing Co., Inc.
1 Dag Hammarskjold Plaza
New York, New York 10017

Dictionnaire le Robert
107 avenue Parmentier
Paris 11, France

Dramatists Play Service, Inc.
440 Park Avenue South
New York, New York 10016

Edelweiss Press
124 Front Street
Massapequa Park, New York 11762

Education Research Associates
Box 767
Amherst, Massachusetts

Educational Solutions
80 Fifth Avenue
New York, New York 10011

Educators Publishing Service
75 Moulton Street
Cambridge, Massachusetts 02138

English Language Services, Inc.
14350 N.W. Science Park Drive
Portland, Oregon 97229

Evans Brothers, Ltd.
Montague House, Russell Square
London WC1B 5BX, England

The Experiment in International Living
Brattleboro, Vermont 05301

Faber and Faber
24 Russell Square
London, England

Samuel French, Inc.
25 West 45th Street
New York, New York 10036

Globe Book Company, Inc.
175 Fifth Avenue
New York, New York 10010

Grove Press, Inc.
196 West Houston Street
New York, New York 10014

Harcourt Brace Jovanovich, Inc.
757 Third Avenue
New York, New York 10017

Harper & Row, Publishers, Inc.
10 East 53rd Street
New York, New York 10022

Harrap and Company, Ltd.
182–184 High Holborn
London WC1V 7AX, England

Hart Publishing Company, Inc.
12 East 12th Street
New York, New York 10003

D. C. Heath & Company
125 Spring Street
Lexington, Massachusetts 02173

Heinle & Heinle Enterprises
29 Lexington Road
Concord, Massachusetts 01742

Holt, Rinehart and Winston, Inc.
383 Madison Avenue
New York, New York 10017

Human Development Training Institute
P.O. Box 1505
La Mesa, California 92401

Institute of Modern Languages, Inc.
2622 Pittman Drive
Silver Spring, Maryland 20910

International Film Bureau, Inc.
332 S.W. Michigan Avenue
Chicago, Illinois 60604

JAB Press, Inc.
P.O. Box 315
Franklin Lakes, New Jersey 07417

Langenscheidt
Neusser Str. 3
8 Munich 40, West Germany

Language Innovations, Inc.
2112 Broadway, Suite 515
New York, New York 10023

Larousse & Co., Inc.
572 Fifth Avenue
New York, New York 10036

Littlefield, Adams and Company
8 Adams Drive
Totowa, New Jersey 07512

Litton Educational Publishing International
135 West 50th Street
New York, New York 10020

Longman, Inc.
19 West 44th Street
New York, New York 10036

Macmillan, Inc.
866 Third Avenue
New York, New York 10022

Charles E. Merrill Publishing Company
1300 Alum Creek Drive
Columbus, Ohio 43216

Modern Language Association of America
62 Fifth Avenue
New York, New York 10011

National Education Association Publishing
1201 16th Street, N.W.
Washington, D.C. 20036

National Humanistic Education Center
110 Spring Street
Saratoga Springs, New York 12866

National Textbook Company
8259 Niles Center Road
Skokie, Illinois 60077

The New American Library, Inc.
1301 Avenue of the Americas
New York, New York 10019

The New Games Foundation
P.O. Box 7901
San Francisco, California 94120

Newbury House, Publishers, Inc.
54 Warehouse Lane
Rowley, Massachusetts 01969

Philadelphia Humanistic Education Center
8504 Germantown Avenue
Philadelphia, Pennsylvania 19118

Pocket Books
Simon and Schuster, Inc.
1230 Avenue of the Americas
New York, New York 10020

Popular Library
A Division of CBS Publications
1515 Broadway
New York, New York 10036

Prentice-Hall, Inc.
Englewood Cliffs, New Jersey 07632

Rand McNally & Company
8255 Central Park Avenue
Skokie, Illinois 60076

Scholastic Book Services
50 West 44th Street
New York, New York 10036

Scott, Foresman and Company
1900 East Lake Avenue
Glenview, Illinois 60025

TESOL
455 Nevils Building
Georgetown University
Washington, D.C. 20057

Teachers' Collaborative
700 Chillingworth Drive
West Palm Beach, Florida 33409

Teachers College Press
1234 Amsterdam Avenue
New York, New York 10027

University of Chicago Press
5801 Ellis Avenue
Chicago, Illinois 60637

The University Press of Hawaii
2840 Kolowalu Street
Honolulu, Hawaii 96822

Verlag für Sprachmethodik
Königswinter am Rhein, West Germany

Voxcom
A Division of Tapecon Inc.
P.O. Box 4741
10 Latta Road
Rochester, New York 14612

Washington Square Press
Simon and Schuster, Inc.
1230 Avenue of the Americas
New York, New York 10020

The Wider Horizons Project
866 United Nations Plaza
New York, New York 10017

Peter H. Wyden, Inc.
750 Third Avenue
New York, New York 10017

Xerox Education Publications
Education Center
1250 Fairwood Avenue
Columbus, Ohio 43216

Appendix B

REPRODUCTION PAGES

To make it quicker and easier to use the activities suggested in the language chapters of this book, we have prepared these Reproduction Pages. They are perforated for easy removal and can be used for either projection or duplication.

1. *For projection with an opaque projector,* no further preparation is necessary. The page is simply inserted in the projector for viewing by the whole class.

2. *For projection with an overhead projector,* the page must be converted into a transparency. To produce the transparency, overlay the Reproduction Page with a blank transparency and run both through a copying machine.

3. *For copying with a spirit duplicator,* a master can be made from the Reproduction Page. Overlay it with a special heat-sensitive spirit master and run both through a copying machine. The spirit master can then be used to reproduce 50 to 100 copies on paper.

Please note that all material appearing on Reproduction Pages, as in the rest of the book, is protected under the United States Copyright Law. Allyn and Bacon, Inc., grants to readers the right to make multiple copies of Reproduction Pages for nonprofit educational use only. All other rights are reserved.

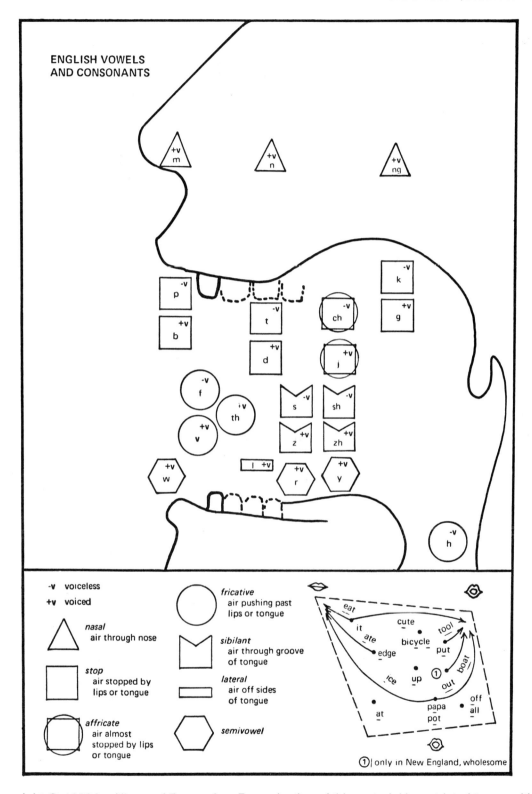

ENGLISH VOWELS AND CONSONANTS

CONSONANTS (1)

The following are consonants made with the lips. Those that are underlined are voiced (vibrated in the throat).

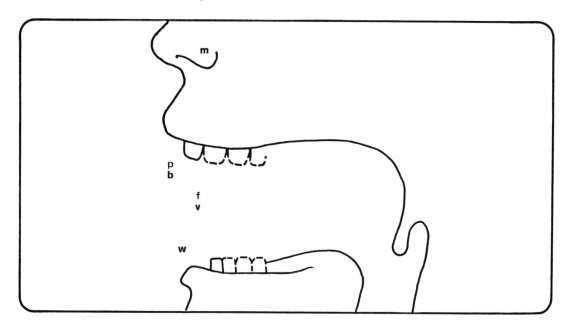

The Letter (Pronunciation)	A Word with the Letter	Other Words with the Same Sound (Perhaps Different Spelling)
<u>m</u> (em)	man	mom,
p (pē)	pen	pop,
<u>b</u> (bē)	book	ball,
f (ef)	four	<u>ph</u>otograph, lau<u>gh</u>ing, five,
<u>v</u> (vē)	five	television,
<u>w</u> (dub'yōō)	woman	wall,

CONSONANTS (2)

The following consonants are made with the tongue against the teeth or just behind the teeth. Those that are underlined are voiced (vibrated in the throat).

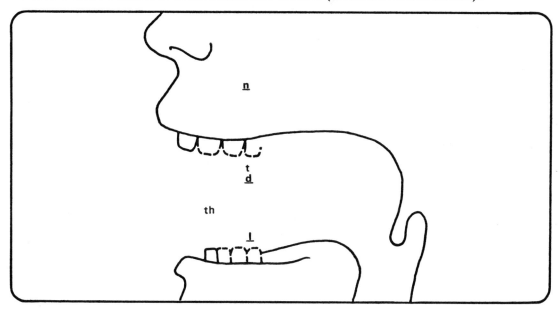

The Letter (Pronunciation)	A Word with the Letter	Other Words with the Same Sound (Perhaps Different Spelling)
<u>n</u> (en)	nose	nine, _____
		_____
t (tē)	teacher	ten, _____
		_____
<u>d</u> (dē)	dog	door, _____
		_____
<u>l</u> (el)	light	ball, _____
		_____
<u>th</u> (tē āch)	this	the, _____
(<u>th</u> written with two letters, but pronounced as one sound, with the tip of the tongue pushed forward between the top and bottom teeth)		_____
th (voiceless)	thanks	things, _____
		_____

CONSONANTS (3)

The following consonants are made with the tongue in the middle of the mouth.
Those that are underlined are voiced (vibrated in the throat).

The Letter (Pronunciation)	A Word with the Letter	Other Words with the Same Sound (Perhaps Different Spelling)
s (es)	six	cents, city, miss, _____
		_____
z (zē)	zero	boys, buzz, _____
		_____
r (är)	red	car, _____
		_____
ch (sē āch) (two letters, one sound)	chair	watch, _____
		_____
j (jā)	jump	ginger, judge, individual, page, _____
		_____
sh (es āch) (two letters, one sound)	shirt	fish, _____
		_____
zh (zē āch) (two letters, one sound, usually spelled si, su)	Zhivago	usually, television, _____
		_____
y (wī)	yes	you, _____
		_____

CONSONANTS (4)

The following consonants are made at the back of the mouth and in the throat. Those that are underlined are voiced (vibrated in the throat).

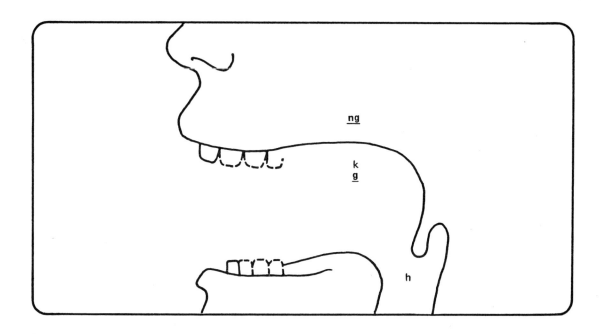

The Letter (Pronunciation)	A Word with the Letter	Other Words with the Same Sound (Perhaps Different Spelling)
<u>ng</u> (en jē) (one sound, two letters)	song	singing,
k (kā)	kilometer	<u>c</u>at, <u>c</u>ute, <u>c</u>oat, bla<u>ck</u>, <u>q</u>ueen,
<u>g</u> (jē)	good	e<u>x</u>am, leg,
h (āch)	home	hel<u>p</u>,

VOWELS (1)

Short vowel sounds in English are different from vowels in most other languages. They are generally more relaxed.

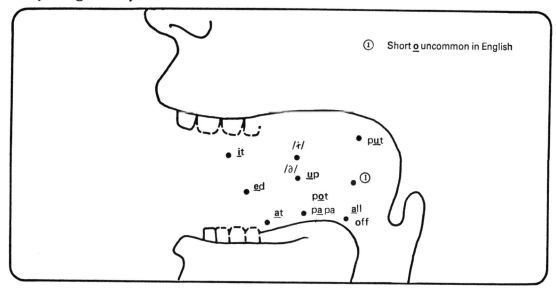

Tongue forward, lips spread | Other Words with the Same Sound

it — sit, is,

edge — red, pencil,

at — cat, black,

Tongue back, lips rounded

put — book, full,

off — all, on,

Tongue middle, lips open and round

papa, pot — top, mama,

up — butter, cup,

Tongue and lips relaxed in unstressed syllables

lion — orange, middle,

(after vowels and voiced consonants)

city — bicycle,

(after voiceless consonants)

VOWELS (2)

Longer vowels are actually diphthongs or glides made by the movement of the tongue and lips from one vowel position toward another.

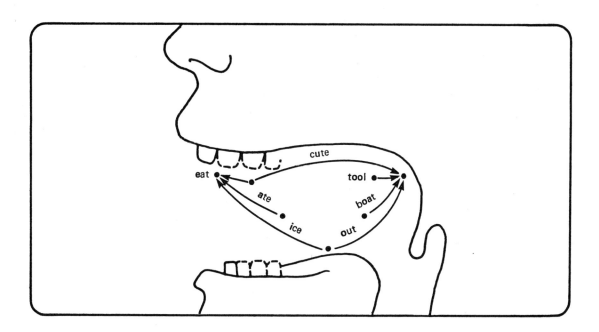

Longer Vowels Glides	Letter	Other Words with the Same Sound
eat	e	please, green,
ate	a	name, table,
ice	i	pie, like,
out	ou	house, brown
boat	o	close, window,
tool	oo	school, blue,
cute	u	united, few, you,

THE VERB BE IN QUESTIONS AND ANSWERS (1)

Fill in all the blank spaces.

3rd person singular, masculine

	(red)	(blue)	(red)	(yellow)	(green)
Yes		He	's		a
		He	is		a
?	Is	he			a
	Isn't	he			a
No		He	is	not	a
		He	's	not	a
		He	is	n't	a

3rd person singular, feminine

Yes		She	's		a
?					
No					

3rd person plural

Yes		They	're		students.
		They	are		
?					
No					

Who?

Yes?		Who	's		a
No?					

THE VERB BE IN QUESTIONS AND ANSWERS (2)

Fill in all the blank spaces.. .. .. ..

2nd person singular

	(red)	(blue)	(red)	(yellow)	(green)
Yes		You	're		a
		You	are		a
?	Are	you			a
	Aren't	you			a
No		You	are	not	a
		You	're	not	a
		You	are	n't	a

2nd person plural

	(red)	(blue)	(red)	(yellow)	(green)
Yes		You	're		students.
?					
No					

1st person plural

	(red)	(blue)	(red)	(yellow)	(green)
Yes		We	're		students.
?					
No					

1st person singular

	(red)	(blue)	(red)	(yellow)	(green)
Yes		I	'm		a student.
?					
	Am	I		not	a student?
No					

MY ROOM

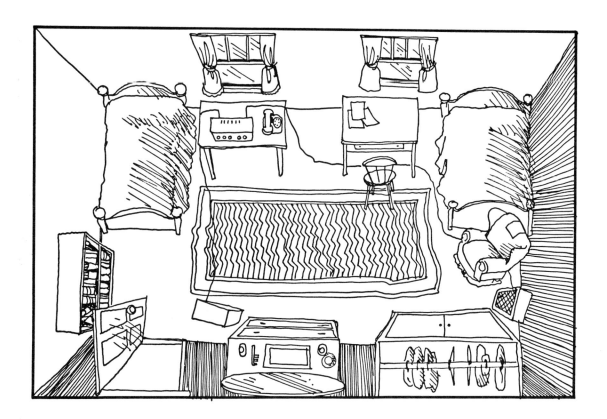

In my room there are two beds. There is a window at the head of each bed. There is a rug on the floor. The desk and chair are between the two beds. The bookcase is at the foot of my bed. The telephone and the stereo are on the table beside the bed. The dresser is near the door next to the closet, and the two speakers are on the floor. It's a nice room!

PLACES AND FEELINGS

Think of places where you are during a typical week and how you feel there. Complete the following sentences.

1. When I'm _____ at school _____ , I'm happy.

   When _____ Tom _____ is _____ at a basketball game, he's happy.

2. When I'm _____, I'm excited.

   When _____ is _____.

3. When I'm _____, I'm contented.

   When _____ is _____.

4. When I'm _____, I'm sad.

   When _____ is _____ .

5. When I'm _____, I'm nervous.

   When _____ is _____.

6. When I'm _____, I'm bored.

   When _____ is _____.

7. When I'm _____, I'm _____.

   When _____ is _____.

8. When I'm _____, I'm _____.

   When _____ is _____.

PRESENT CONTINUOUS BABY

WHAT ARE YOU DOING?

Fill in the missing word.

I'm _____ through the woods.

I'm _____ television.

I'm _____ on a stool.

I'm _____ by a lamppost.

I'm _____ a small dog.

I'm _____ a magazine.

Copy these sentences in the order of your preference of the activity involved.

1. _____.
2. _____.
3. _____.
4. _____.
5. _____.
6. _____.

WHO ARE YOU?

1. Who are you?

    I'm a _____.   **We're** _____.

    I'm not a _____.   **We're not** _____.

2. Where are you?

    I'm _____.   **We're** _____.

    I'm not _____.   **We're not** _____.

3. What are you doing?

    I'm _____.   **We're** _____.

    I'm not _____.   **We're not** _____.

4. How are you?

    I'm _____.   **We're** _____.

    I'm not _____.   **We're not** _____.

AN IMAGINARY TRIP

Describe your imaginary trip to a small group of classmates.

1. Where are you going to go?

2. How are you going to go?

3. When are you going to go?

4. With whom are you going to go?

5. How long are you going to stay?

6. What are you going to do there?

7. Where are you going to live?

8. Are you going to work?

9. Are you going to have a lot of free time?

10. Are you going to read a lot?

11. What are you going to take with you?

12. Are you going to buy a lot of new things for the trip?

13. What are you going to miss at school?

14. To whom are you going to write?

15. Who is going to miss you?

16. Whom are you going to miss?

A FAMILY TREE

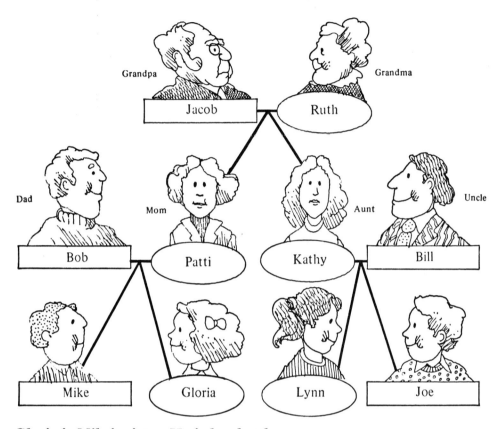

Gloria is Mike's sister. He is her brother.

She is Bob's and Patti's daughter. They are her parents.

Gloria is Ruth's and Jacob's granddaughter. They are her grandparents.

She is Kathy's and Bill's niece. They are her aunt and uncle.

She is Lynn's and Joe's cousin. They are her cousins.

Draw your own family tree. Describe it like this:

I am ___Gloria___ .

I am ___Mike's___ sister. He is my brother.

I am . . . .
Continue!

THE AUXILIARY VERB "DO"

Fill in the blank spaces.

3rd person singular, masculine

	(red)	(blue)	(red)	(yellow)	(orange)
Yes		He			works.
?	Does	he			work?
	Doesn't	he			work?
No		He	does	not	work.
		He	does	n't	work.

3rd person singular, feminine

Yes		She			works.
?					
No					

3rd person plural

Yes		They			work.
?	Do				
	Don't				
No					

Add a tag question to each *Yes* or *No* statement above and answer it with a short sentence. Example:

He works, doesn't he?
Yes, he does./ No, he doesn't.

He doesn't work, does he?
Yes, he does./ No, he doesn't.

THE AUXILIARY VERB "DO"

Fill in all the blank spaces.

2nd person singular or plural

	(red)	(blue)	(red)	(yellow)	(orange)
Yes	░░░	You	░░░	░░░	work.
?			░░░	░░░	
			░░░	░░░	
No	░░░				

1st person singular

Yes	░░░	I	░░░	░░░	work.
?			░░░	░░░	
			░░░	░░░	
No	░░░				

1st person plural

Yes	░░░	We	░░░	░░░	work.
?			░░░	░░░	
			░░░	░░░	
No	░░░				

Complete these short statements.

Yes, you do. Yes, I _____ . Yes, we _____ .

No, you _____ . No, I _____ . No, we _____ .

FIND SOMEONE WHO . . .

Walk around and ask people questions in order to find someone who . . . .

1. plays tennis.

   Do you play tennis?
   _____John_____ plays tennis.

2. talks a lot.

   Do you _____a lot?
   _____

3. frequently goes camping.

   _____?
   _____

4. laughs a lot.

   _____?
   _____

5. seldom tells jokes.

   Do you often _____?
   _____

6. dances.

   _____?
   _____

7. usually wears blue jeans.

   _____?
   _____

8. always locks the door at night.

   _____?
   _____

9. seldom watches T.V.

   _____?
   _____

10. often eats in restaurants.

    _____?
    _____

WHAT DO YOU DO?

1. Do you watch television very much? What is one of your favorite programs?

2. Do you read a lot? What do you read?

3. Do you think that grades help you to learn?

4. What are you going to do during the next vacation?

5. Do you learn more in school or outside of school?

6. Do your parents buy records? What kind of records do they buy? Do you buy records?

7. How do you get money to spend?

8. Do you know what you want to do some day?

9. Do you celebrate Thanksgiving or Christmas? How do you celebrate them?

10. Do you work? Where do you work?

11. Do you smoke? Do you want to quit smoking?

12. Do you often go to museums? What kind of museums do you go to?

13. Where do you listen to music?

14. Do you go to concerts? With whom?

15. Do you know how to ski? Do you want to learn?

16. Do you know how to play the guitar? Do you want to learn?

17. Do you know the director of the school?

18. Do you or does someone in your family know a famous person?

19. Who knows you very well?

20. Do you give many parties?

21. Do you go to many parties? Do you dance?

22. Do you study alone or with friends?

23. Do you write letters? To whom do you write?

A PEOPLE HUNT

Walk around asking questions like the following in order to find someone who likes a particular thing:

Do you like ice cream?

Do you like to swim?

Complete each sentence with the name of a different person.

1. _____ likes ice cream.

2. _____ likes chocolates.

3. _____ likes cheese.

4. _____ likes strawberries.

5. _____ likes to cook.

6. _____ likes to go fishing.

7. _____ likes to paint.

8. _____ likes to swim.

9. _____ likes to go camping.

10. _____ likes school.

TEN THINGS I LIKE TO DO

	My parents like to do it.		Initial	$$$
	Mother	Father	Cost	Each Time
1.				
2.				
3.				
4.				
5.				
6.				
7.				
8.				
9.				
10.				

WHO ARE YOU?

Put a check mark next to any statement that you feel describes you.

1. _____ am quiet.
2. _____ like to be alone.
3. _____ talk a lot.
4. _____ am a good listener.
5. _____ likc to go camping.
6. _____ like sports.
7. _____ like to learn new things.
8. _____ like to sing.
9. _____ like to dance.
10. _____ like to draw or paint.
11. _____ like to make things.
12. _____ read a lot.
13. _____ never read unless I have to.
14. _____ enjoy arguing.
15. _____ do anything to avoid an argument.
16. _____ like to laugh.
17. _____ like advice from my friends.
18. _____ like advice from my teachers.
19. _____ like to give advice.
20. _____ like to talk things out.
21. _____ am easy to get along with.
22. _____ fight when I don't like something.
23. _____ think people are fun to be with.
24. _____ am friendly.
25. _____ usually like what I am doing.
26. _____ know how to make things interesting for myself.
27. _____ don't feel happy until my work is done.
28. _____ tell jokes.
29. _____ am bored easily.
30. _____ can be trusted.
31. _____ like to correct others.
32. _____ help others with their work.
33. _____ like to tell others what to do.

A BAD DAY

A BAD DAY (2)

CHILDHOOD

1. When you were a child, where did you live?

2. Did you live in the country or in the city?

3. Did you sleep upstairs or downstairs?

4. Did you share your bedroom with anyone?

5. Did you play ball?

6. Did you play with dolls?

7. What games did you play?

8. Did you like school?

9. Did you study a lot?

10. Did lots of people visit your family?

11. Did you learn a lot at school?

12. Did you play a musical instrument?

13. Did you practice a lot?

14. Did you visit your grandparents?

16. Where did they live?

17. Did you watch television?

18. Did you earn money? How?

19. What did you want to be when you grew up?

20. How many people lived in your house?

21. What was your best friend's name?

HOW WAS YOUR FIELD TRIP?

1. How did you decide with whom to go? Did you decide to go alone, be with friends, go with people you didn't know at all? Explain.

2. Write a summary of what you did. How did you go? With whom? What did you do there?

3. Thinking about your experience, complete these sentences.

When _____ I felt _____.

When _____ I felt _____.

When _____ I felt _____.

When _____ I felt _____.

When _____ I felt _____.

4. What did you do for the first time? How did you feel?

5. What did you want to do differently: talk to more people, be there longer, be more involved? Why didn't you do it?

6. Make a list of seven words that you associate with the place where you went.

7. Pick one or two of the following sentences to finish.

I learned that _____.

I was surprised that _____.

I remembered that _____.

I relearned that _____.

I realized that _____.

I observed that _____.

DO YOU WANT IT?

Fill in appropriate questions and your answers.

1. **I would like to give you a guitar. Do you want it?**
   No, thank you, I don't want it.

2. **I would like to give you some flowers. Do you want them?**
   Yes, give them to me please.

3. **I would like to give you a water bed.** _____ **?**
   _____ **.**

4. **I would like to give you some cookies.** _____ **?**
   _____ **.**

5. **I would like to give you a sports car.** _____ **?**
   _____ **.**

6. **I would like to give you a Spanish dictionary.** _____ **?**
   _____ **.**

7. **I would like to give you an English dictionary.** _____ **?**
   _____ **.**

8. **I would like to give you some new skis.** _____ **?**
   _____ **.**

9. **I would like to give you a motorcycle.** _____ **?**
   _____ **.**

10. **I would like to give you a ten-speed bike.** _____ **?**
    _____ **.**

11. **I would like to give you some vitamins.** _____ **?**
    _____ **.**

12. **I would like to give you a hamburger.** _____ **?**
    _____ **.**

COMPARISONS

Walk around the room, talking to other students and making comparisons. Write answers to the questions using as many students' names as possible.

1. Who is taller than you are?   _____ is taller than I am.

2. Who is as tall as you?   _____.

3. Who is shorter than you   _____.

4. Who is stronger than you are?   _____.

5. Who is happier than you are today?   _____.

6. Who is more active than you are?   _____.

7. Who is studying more than you are in this class?   _____.

8. Who talks more often in English than you do?   _____.

9. Who is more daring than you are?   _____.

10. Who is more careful than you are?   _____.

11. Who is as dependable as you are?   _____.

HOW DO YOU FEEL?

embarrassed	peaceful	inferior	joyful
frustrated	relaxed	weak	refreshed
nervous	guilty	strong	foolish
grateful	stimulated	free	happy
proud	pressured	envious	inadequate
scared	inspired	defeated	adventuresome
amazed	enthusiastic	tense	bored
angry	lonely	apathetic	boring
annoyed	healthy	sympathetic	cold
ashamed	energetic	confident	warm
excited	confused	timid	friendly
good	accepted	shy	cautious
furious	contented	brave	creative
sad	thrilled	courageous	capable
unhappy	responsible	daring	serious
depressed	indebted	generous	loving
humble _ n ool st	overwhelmed	clumsy	caring
calm	relieved	worthless	careful
patient	satisfied	stupid	dependable
impatient	superior	triumphant	confident
secure	insecure	loved	irritable

WHAT WILL YOU BE LIKE?

Answer "yes," or "no," or "probably" to each question.

1. Will you have six children or more?
2. Will you marry someone of a different religion?
3. Will you ever stop smoking?
4. Will you ever grow a beard? (*male*)
5. Will you ever date a man with a beard? (*female*)
6. Will you always read the sports in the newspaper?
7. Will you marry for money?
8. Will you graduate from college?
9. Will you earn a lot of money?
10. Will you be boss in your family?
11. Will you live here always?
12. Will you travel in space?
13. Will you travel to other countries?
14. Will you learn another language?
15. Will you ever smoke?
16. Will you have a big wedding?
17. Will you get fat?
18. Will you watch a lot of television when you are forty years old?
19. Will you invite people of a different race to your house?
20. Will you live on a street with people of a different race?
21. Will you marry more than once?
22. Will you surely move away from your home town?
23. Will you ever have a car?
24. Will you have trouble with the police?
25. Will you drive very fast?
26. Will you be a good father or mother?
27. Will you frequently get drunk?
28. Will you get very angry with your husband or wife?
29. Will you always go away for vacations?
30. Will you stay at home every evening?
31. Will you work after marriage?

FUTURE

In five years . . .

 1. What year will it be?
 2. How old will you be?
 3. Will you be living near here?
 4. Will you be married?
 5. Will you have any children?
 6. Will you have the same job?
 7. What kind of a job will you have?
 8. What kind of a job would you like to have?
 9. Will you be able to afford a car, a house?
10. Will you have a lot of money in the bank?
11. Will we have a Republican, Democratic, or third-party president?
12. Will the president be black? Will the president be a woman?
13. Will you be afraid of the end of the world, a civil war, or a nuclear war?
14. Will there be enough to eat in the world?
15. Will you be a vegetarian?
16. What will be the big news in the headlines?
17. How much will you pay for a loaf of bread?
18. Will cars run on gas?
19. Will every family have a plane? Will it be a jet?
20. Will we have robots?
21. Will we eat dehydrated food and capsules instead of fresh food?
22. How will ecology affect the way of life?
23. Will all clothing be unisex?
24. Will the earth be governed by an international institution?
25. Will we have shortages?
26. Will you have a computer in your home?

MODAL VERBS

Fill in the blank spaces.

Willingness	*(red)*	*(blue)*	*(red)*	*(yellow)*	*(orange)*
Yes		He	'll		cook
		He	will		cook
?	Will	he			cook?
	Won't	he			cook?
No		He	will	not	cook.
		He	wo	n't	cook.

Less sure willingness					
Yes		He	'd		come.
?					
	Wouldn't	he			go?
No					

Escapable obligation or duty					
Yes					
		He	should		go.
?					
No					

Inescapable obligation (has to) Mustn't *is often replaced by* doesn't have to.					
Yes					
		He	must		work.
?					
	*				
No					
			*		

CHAPTER 2, ACTIVITY 15.8

Ability or permission

Yes	░	░	░	░	
	░	He	can	░	swim.
?			░	░	
			░	░	
No	░				
	░				

Add a tag question to each *Yes* or *No* statement above and answer it with a short sentence. Example:

He'll cook, won't he?
Yes, he will. / No, he won't.

He won't cook, will he?
Yes, he will. / No, he won't.

WHAT CAN YOU DO WELL?

Answer these questions, then discuss the questions in groups of three or four.

1. What can you do well? (*Name several things.*)

2. What should you do today? (*Name several things.*)

3. What must you do today?

4. What would you like to do today?

5. How do you feel when you should do something, but you can't do it well?

6. How do you feel when you should do something but you would like to do something else?

7. Is there something that you should do, that you would like to do, and that you can do well? How do you feel when you are doing that?

PRINCIPAL PARTS OF IRREGULAR VERBS

Unfortunately, English is highly irregular. You'll find some patterns, but you'll have to learn them through usage.

1. The present tense, the past tense, and the past participle are the same.

cut	cut	cut
hit	hit	hit
hurt	hurt	hurt
let	let	let
put	put	put
quit	quit	quit
set	set	set
shut	shut	shut
split	split	split

2. The past tense and past participle are the same, but different from the present tense.

build	built	built
sit	sat	sat
send	sent	sent
spend	spent	spent

feed	fed	fed
hold	held	held
read	read	read
		(pronounced / red/)

feel	felt	felt
keep	kept	kept
leave	left	left
mean	meant	meant
meet	met	met
sleep	slept	slept
sweep	swept	swept

bring	brought	brought
catch	caught	caught
fight	fought	fought
seek	sought	sought
teach	taught	taught
think	thought	thought

bind	bound	bound
find	found	found
grind	ground	ground

get	got	got(ten)
lose	lost	lost
shoot	shot	shot

hear	heard	heard
lay	laid	laid
pay	paid	paid
make	made	made
say	said	said
sell	sold	sold
stand	stood	stood

hang	hung	hung
stick	stuck	stuck
sting	stung	stung
strike	struck	struck
swing	swung	swung
win	won	won

CHAPTER 2, ACTIVITY 16.6

3. The present tense, the past tense, and the past participle are all different.

break	broke	broken
choose	chose	chosen
freeze	froze	frozen
speak	spoke	spoken
steal	stole	stolen
weave	wove	woven

swear	swore	sworn
tear	tore	torn
wear	wore	worn

blow	blew	blown
draw	drew	drawn
grow	grew	grown
know	knew	known
throw	threw	thrown

eat	ate	eaten
fall	fell	fallen
give	gave	given
shake	shook	shaken
take	took	taken

ride	rode	ridden
rise	rose	risen
write	wrote	written

bite	bit	bitten
hide	hid	hidden

do	did	done
fly	flew	flown
go	went	gone
lie	lay	lain
see	saw	seen

drink	drank	drunk
ring	rang	rung
shrink	shrank	shrunk
sing	sang	sung
sink	sank	sunk
spring	sprang	sprung
stink	stank	stunk
swim	swam	swum

4. The present tense and past participle are the same, but the past tense is different.

become	became	become
come	came	come
run	ran	run

VERBS IN THE PAST

Fill in the appropriate blanks.

Present perfect: something that has happened at some indefinite period in the past, any time up to the present moment.

	(red)	(blue)	(red)	(yellow)	(orange)	(green)
Yes		I	've		eaten	fish.
		I	have		played	volley ball.
?	Have	I			eaten	bean sprouts?
	Haven't	I			played	tennis?
No		I	have	n't		
		I	have	not		

Simple past: something that happened at a specific past time.

Yes						
		I			caught	a fish
?	Did	I				
No						

Past progressive: an incomplete activity or series of acts in the past.

Yes						
		I	was		writing	a letter.
?						
No						

GRANDPARENTS

1. Are your grandparents living?

2. Where do they or did they live?

3. Did they always live there? If not, where did they live before?

4. What language did they speak when they were children?

5. What languages did they learn?

6. What kind of work did they do?

7. What kind of interesting things have they done?

8. To which of your grandparents do or did you feel closest?

9. Have you spent much time with your grandparents?

10. How much influence have they had on your life?

AM I CREATIVE?

1. Within the last six months, have you tried anything different? Have you made any change in your relationship with anyone? Have you made anything? Have you had a new idea?

2. Can you think of any experience in your childhood that has helped you try new things? Can you think of any experience that made you believe you can't do certain things?

3. Has there been anyone who encouraged you to do new things or who discouraged you from doing new things?

4. What are you going to do different this month or this year?

5. Can you think of something you have accomplished that was difficult?

WHAT WOULD YOU DO?

	Would your parents do the same?	
	Mother	*Father*
1. If you were driving at night and saw someone in trouble, what would you do?		
2. If a friend gave you the answers for an exam, what would you do?		
3. If a teacher gave you a zero on an exam, accusing you unjustly of having cheated, what would you do?		
4. If you bought something and found it defective when you got home, what would you do?		
5. If you had a million dollars, what kind of house would you have?		
6. If the government chose you to go to another planet, would you go?		
7. If you had graduated from high school last year, would you be studying at a university now?		
8. If someone were to give you a scholarship to go to a particular university but you didn't like the university, would you accept the scholarship and would you go?		
9. If you could be successful at one thing, what would you do?		
10. If you found out tonight that you were going to move to another city, how would you feel?		

Appendix C

FEEDBACK FORM

Good luck!

We are eager to have you start. We are Interested In hearing about your experiences with your classes. If you have any corrections or suggestions for a new edition of this book, please let us know. For convenience, there is a form on the following page.

We look forward to hearing from you and we promise to send you a reply.

Virginia Wilson and
   Beverly Wattenmaker
c/o Longwood Division
Allyn and Bacon, Inc.
470 Atlantic Avenue
Boston, Massachusetts 02210

Dear Ginny and Bev:

I want to tell you what I think about *A Guidebook for Teaching Foreign Language.* I like certain things about the book, including:

I do, however, feel that the book could be improved in the following ways:

There are some things I wish the book had included, such as:

Here is something that happened in my class when I used an idea from your book:

                                                         Sincerely yours,

                                         _____

School: _____
Address: _____
City and State: _____
Date: _____